THE SHOCK OF REVELATION

THE SHOCK OF REVELATION

Alexander Stewart

THE SEABURY PRESS
New York

Copyright © 1967 by The Seabury Press, Inc.
Library of Congress Catalog Card Number: 67-11469
Design by Nancy H. Dale
552-C-1166-4
Printed in the United States of America

Scriptural quotations, unless otherwise noted, are from the Authorized Version of the Bible.

ACKNOWLEDGMENTS

Grateful acknowledgment is made to the following publishers and authors for permission to use copyrighted material from the titles listed below:

Harcourt, Brace & World, Inc.—T. S. Eliot, "Murder in the Cathedral," Part I, *The Complete Poems and Plays of T. S. Eliot.*

Harper & Row, Publishers, Inc.—G. A. Studdert-Kennedy, *The Best of G. A. Studdert-Kennedy,* copyrighted 1948 by Harper & Brothers. Used by permission.

Holt, Rinehart & Winston, Inc.—Prayer by John Ward, quoted by Martin C. D'Arcy, S.J., in *The Mind and Heart of Love.*

PROLOGUE

Shock—impact—is a phenomenon familiar to our world. Insulin and electric shock are used in medicine. Contemporary art is often designed to shock the beholder. Journalism selects the shocking word or phrase that will make an impact. Likewise, in the realm of religion, revelation can be shocking.

The shock of revelation, the moment of insight, is called in psychology the "aha" moment of awareness when the response to light breaking through is invariably, "Aha, now I see." The perplexed ninth-grader, for example, certain that he can never master algebra, suddenly understands the principle of inversion and beams with joy.

Revelation often bursts upon us unexpectedly. It may come through intellect, our aesthetic faculties, intuition, emotion, or through the mystical impulse. When revelation occurs in the realm of emotion, it may be highly suspect. Yet revelation can be lasting and lead to sound decision precisely because it has moved us deeply. Revelation is not a flight from reason, but rather supplements and transcends it. The Christian is not forced to choose between reason and revelation but may utilize both for richness and balance.

Through revelation, Christ becomes a vivid reality in our lives. We sense that God has broken through into this universe in the Person of Christ. We become aware that Christ's act on the Cross has personal implications. We may realize that the Resurrection makes possible life in another dimension even while we are still earthbound.

The shock of revelation is a stepping stone toward religious maturity. Some encounter it at a relatively young age; for others an episode in life, a Niagara moment, hastens its advent; while for still others it may be the "flame-lit revelation," the searing inner vision. When this seemingly indescribable experience does occur, we borrow the poet's phrase, "Thou crystal Christ."

In the pages that follow, the essence of the Gospel is set forth, misconceptions of religion are examined, and the Person of Jesus Christ is presented so that men caught in the human predicament may encounter Him, become committed to Him, and share the excitement of living with Him.

CONTENTS

THE SHOCK OF REVELATION

1

NIAGARA MOMENTS

Shortly before midnight on March 29, 1848, a farmer in upstate New York took his late evening stroll. He absorbed the scented spring atmosphere, found new forms in scenes he had passed many times. Suddenly an uneasy feeling possessed him. Something was wrong. What was it? He could not single it out. His uneasiness became anxiety; his anxiety soon turned into terror when he realized that the familiar sound of nearby Niagara Falls was absent. Perhaps he was becoming deaf? No, he could hear the crackle of twigs underfoot. Maybe an unusual southerly wind was carrying the noise northward? He rushed ahead, arriving at the falls breathless and horror stricken.

Mighty Niagara had stopped! Why so suddenly? Was the world coming to an end? The farmer dashed home. His family scoffed until they too sensed the absence of the echoes of churning water and smashing force. Next morning, Buffalo, Rochester, and Syracuse newspapers carried banner headlines. People panicked. By afternoon, over ten thousand gaped at the dried-up river bed; some even walked across. Prayer vigils began at nightfall to coerce the Almighty into resuming the flow of water. Was the world coming to an end? Surely this was the sign, some said. Thirty hours later, as suddenly as they had stopped, the falls resumed their terrible torrent.[1]

I am not concerned with the scientific explanation of such an event, although there is one, but propose that it is a parable of human experience. Every life

3

has its Niagara moments when, for thirty minutes, thirty hours, thirty days, even thirty years, life seems to have come to a halt. The thunder of Niagara—be it the honking of horns, the blare of TV, or the rush, tension, and din of modern life—renders us deaf to the silence of the spirit and kills any chance for deep inner reflection. When the silence comes, we suddenly have to face ourselves.

For some, Niagara moments strike with sudden tragedy: an accident, a drowning, a heart attack, an unexpected event. To others, Niagara moments come when the bottom drops out of life: when the worker is told after forty years, "We won't need your services any longer"; when the parents discover that in spite of their efforts and money, Junior did poorly on the college boards; when the young girl discovers herself both pregnant and deserted; when the jury foreman declares, "We have reached a verdict, your honor." Niagara moments may come in the form of mental depression, negative feelings about the futility of life, or when a broken heart and wounded spirit set us brooding.

How do we face our Niagara moments? Some people panic, like the residents of the Niagara area, never asking the scientific HOW or the religious WHY. Disruption of order is so upsetting that they cannot think clearly. Others rebel, accusing God or someone of being at fault—the other driver, the lifeguard, the doctor. Many are stunned, lost; they can't believe it. They want assurance that the event isn't true, that they are in a daydream. A few use their Niagara moments, see through the tragedy, or find a new basis for living or a belief that answers the ultimate WHY.

What does this have to do with the Christian faith? On the Cross, Jesus exclaimed, "My God, my God, why hast Thou forsaken me?" (Matt. 27:46

RSV). For forty hours thereafter, life stood still. Then came the Resurrection. Life began again on a different level. During the interim, He descended into hell so that He might share and understand our Niagara moments of deepest despair. Jesus had His Niagara moments—in the wilderness, in the garden, on the Cross. Through our baptism we are buried with Him on Good Friday so that having descended into hell, having passed through our Niagara moments, we can share in His Resurrection. God on occasion withdraws momentarily to put us on our own, to test our mettle.

In anguish a person cries, "It is not fair! It is not fair!"—the man sentenced to prison unjustly, the good mother of a murderous son, the innocent girl misled and betrayed, the woman crying for the child she cannot have. Some cry in anger, some in scorn, some brokenly submissive, but all in darkness asking, "Why?"—the question no mortal can answer. It needs a cross to meet it, a Christ to bear it. Unlike the naïve proponents of the cult of easy happiness, Christianity does not explain away the torture of human life to prove that it is just and fair. That would be heartless mockery. Christianity is realistic. It views the Cross and exclaims: "There in that wounded body is the history of the world, the story of man's life on earth. As terrible and tragic as that. But look up, beyond the Cross to the Christ. There is the meaning and purpose of it all."

Niagara moments may seem more difficult than necessary because of our mistaken ideas about the world. Examine just four:

Man has conquered and subdued nature. Has he? Or has he simply learned to obey the laws of nature? If we use the material world as though we own it, every fresh blessing will become a curse. Every new power can become a source of weakness. The machine can become a master instead of a servant. Space travel can enable us to explore God's created world or be an imperialistic opportunity to place our country's flag on the moon and initiate interplanetary warfare. The wonders and blessings of psychology can heal the twisted and tortured mind or be exploited to sell soap, cigarettes, and sex. Do the advertisers understand our motives better than we do?

It doesn't make any difference what you believe. It's what you are that matters. People have been known to say that. How shallow can they be? No mistake about it, belief determines action. Beliefs are powerful; religion is dangerous, a dynamite that can lift us to heaven or drive us to hell. When misused, religion can be as damaging or destructive to the individual or society as no religion at all. What we believe will determine how we will act.

The Bible is a delightful book for children, but rather simple for adults. How can children even begin to comprehend its deep message? The Bible, the record of human history, explores the depths and ascends the heights, reveals not only man's sin but God's redemption, not only Judas' betrayal but Christ's forgiveness. What a Book! Only for children?

Everlasting life begins when you die. On the contrary, it begins here in the present. True, we must die on Good Friday with Christ and go through our Niagara moments to arise a different man, but eternal life begins now.

Such false notions of religion accentuate our Niagara moments. What then is the Christian faith? The record of a Man who *was born uniquely, grew normally, lived perfectly, was crucified commonly, and rose triumphantly.* The acts of Christ's earthly life were the expression in time of His eternal nature. He brought to people a new understanding of creation, the agony of crucifixion, the joy of resurrection, an ascension to a higher level, a conviction of contact with ultimate reality, a vision of the meaning of life.

This man Jesus upsets us. Just as we are about to assert our rights and claim our position, He asks awkward questions as to whether our rights are right, whether we have any position to flaunt. "Don't look at me that way, Jesus. Let me live just a little longer for myself. Go away. I will cover up my deceit, my murders, my lies, and decently disguise my robbery and theft. Go away! My sins aren't so awful. Why do You torment me?" His wounded hands and piercing look compel us to make a decision. If we use God's world for a playground or a battlefield, there will be darkness over the earth from the sixth to the ninth hour, which may be a thousand years, or darkness in our souls for thirty hours or thirty years or a lifetime. Follow our foolish follies, the clouds will darken, life will certainly stop, and then we will have the gall to ask, "Why?"

In our Niagara moments we sense the inadequacy of that on which we have relied for our status. How hollow is that American goddess PERSONAL SUCCESS, as some have discovered:

> The businessman who achieves riches and misses wealth.

> The playboy who attains pleasure and loses happiness.

> The politician who procures power but fails to produce.

The beautiful woman who is admired by everyone but loved by no one.

The overprivileged child showered with presents but devoid of parents.

The cynic who knows the price of everything and the value of nothing.

The cheerful cherub whose brave front of gaiety hides deep insecurity.

In our Niagara moments we realize our insufficiency. Then it is from Christ that we receive *order out of chaos, sense out of nonsense, sanity out of madness.*

Do we know the cause of that mysterious occurrence at Niagara? Just a few miles above the falls, at the mouth of the Niagara River, chunks of ice from Lake Erie welded themselves into a solid block, like ice cubes in a bowl, and prevented the flow of water. No one, in his panic and rebellion, investigated the reason. How often in our Niagara moments do we panic and fret and rebel and weep instead of asking the scientific HOW or the religious WHY? Even on Good Friday the disciples were stunned, dismayed; some questioned whether their loyalty had been ill-placed. Peter wondered if he should get the nets out of storage. Judas committed suicide. If only Judas had waited, he would have discovered that even for a betrayer, life is worth living. The Christian faith is concrete about life, realistic about suffering, triumphant over death. Thirty hours, thirty days, thirty years of Niagara moments cannot defeat the Christian, for he looks beyond the Cross of suffering to the tomb of triumph.

2

TOO BUSY TO HEED

Fifteen hundred people drowned! And yet the tragedy did not have to occur. Five times within two hours their ship had received danger signals. Finally a radio operator from a nearby vessel, the *Californian*, made one last attempt to warn of impending danger from icebergs. The *Titanic* would not listen. Instead, this message was sent: "SHUT UP, I AM BUSY. I AM WORKING THE CAPE RACE." Within a few minutes the mighty *Titanic*, the pride of the oceans, struck an iceberg and within four hours fifteen hundred people perished.

The radio operators on the *Titanic* were too occupied with the highly profitable business of sending and receiving telegrams for the passengers to worry about icebergs on April 14, 1912. Since the builders claimed the *Titanic* was impregnable, unsinkable, why be concerned? Thus the warning signals were ignored while telegrams about the progress of ships in the Cape Sailing Regatta continued to be exchanged. That is, they continued until the ship crashed into the mountain of ice, radio contact was lost, and rescue operations became impossible.

Shut up. I am busy. I am working the Cape Race. We hear that so often: from a businessman headed for ulcers, from a housewife on the verge of a nervous breakdown, from a schoolboy more concerned with sports than with studies, from a young girl "licking the devil's broth." Yet the world of nature and people has been created as a friend, not an enemy. The law of centrifugal force cautions when we are taking a curve too fast; the law of organic change or the "wisdom of the body" warns when we are going to have an upset stomach or a heart attack; the temperature tells when we ought to be wearing a coat or rubbers; and our friends admonish us, sometimes by kidding, that we ought to take it easy. Yet our familiar answer is, "Shut up. I am busy. I am working the Cape Race," or whatever excuse, valid or otherwise, seems suitable.

So many people—especially the man in the mirror—are too busy to heed warnings. Too devoted to the market index to notice the pulse of family unhappiness. Too absorbed in the business of the world to think about the world of the spirit. Self-made men who worship their maker and certainly don't need any advice. "No, thank you, I can take care of myself." Or, "Shut up. I am busy. I am working the Cape Race."

Think of those people who, when they were commanded by our Lord to follow Him, made hasty excuses. "I have to bury my father." "I have to say goodbye to some weekend guests." "I have just bought a new ox [or was it a sports car?] let me first go and try it out." They might just as well have answered, "Shut up. I am busy. I am working the Cape Race." One rich young businessman was so excited about his wealth and success that he told his foreman, "Tear down the old warehouses; let us build bigger and better barns. Business is booming." He looked at his bank book and smiled, "Soul, thou hast much . . . laid up." And our Lord commented, "Thou fool, this night thy soul shall be required of thee" (Luke 12:19-20).

We take years to learn by experience what others could tell us in minutes. How tragic! In our self-assertion, our desire to stand on our own, we waste much talent and energy. We accept willingly the physical inventions from the cave man to the Schweppes man, from fire to filter tips, but in the emotional realm we insist on learning from experience and this retards our progress. We just won't believe that when a sign says WET PAINT, it's wet— as we reach for a tissue to dry our fingers. Men who have attained the heights invariably began where their predecessors left off. They heeded the danger signals.

Jesus aroused people to the danger lurking in unsuspected places. He warned the Pharisees that by allowing legalism to replace love, their religion was doomed to disappear. He exposed the temple authorities as religious racketeers who had prostituted the Hebrew religion by making the synagogue into a gambling den and penny arcade. He disturbed the political leaders when He became the acknowledged leader of a large group of people; the authorities knew that His power came not from numbers or might, but from His Personhood, and such leadership is difficult to purge.

The passengers on the *Titanic* were in love with things. They couldn't have cared less if you had mentioned "salvation," which was what the message might have brought. They were enjoying themselves in the ballroom, the bar, and the banquet halls. The people of Palestine were no different. They were enjoying themselves. Why bother with another messiah bringing salvation? That is why Jesus' body was whipped and bruised. People wanted a messiah who would bring them things and more things: lower taxes, better highways, streamlined horses and chariots, cheap labor from other lands, new perfumes, exotic foods. They wanted things; and all Jesus had to give them was God. So He was crucified. They couldn't be both-

ered with someone who came to warn that their
souls were in mortal danger, so they shouted, "Crucify Him! Crucify Him!" Or, to put it in more recent terms, "Shut up. I am busy. I am working the
Cape Race!"

Jesus asked His followers, "Can ye not discern
the signs of the times?" (Matt. 16:3). Do you
know what the Government budget is for this year?
Or how many displaced persons still await entry
into our country? Or even what happened at the
last meeting of your school committee? When it
comes to "discerning the signs of the times," do we
differ from the citizens of Palestine?

This can be dangerous. As the passengers on the
Titanic discovered, one man's greed can cause another man's death. The people of Palestine discovered that by their unconcern they had killed the
Very Son of God, and Pontius Pilate unwittingly
wrote himself into the creeds of the centuries, a
paradoxical kind of political fame.

As Jesus looked down over the city that day before His triumphal entry, His words are recorded,
"If thou hadst known, even thou, at least in this thy
day, the things which belong unto thy peace! But
now they are hid from thine eyes. For the days shall
come upon thee, that thine enemies shall cast a
trench about thee, and compass thee round, and keep
thee in on every side, and shall lay thee even with
the ground, and thy children within thee; and they
shall not leave in thee one stone upon another; because thou knewest not the time of thy visitation"
(Luke 19:42-44).

"Because thou knewest not the time of thy visitation." People who are unaware that their salvation is upon them are likely to miss salvation or the
Saviour when He comes. As a modern parable, assume that we are notified of Jesus' second coming,

and we rush to the railroad station. After the passengers leave the train, the crowds and celebrities turn away, disappointed that He didn't appear. While all the time Jesus is standing there on the platform in the form of a servant, carrying the baggage for others as He indeed carried a rugged cross on the dusty hill of Calvary centuries ago. A person walking away says, "I guess He must have missed the train." And Jesus whispers, "No, my son, you missed the train."

The radio operator of the *Californian* is trying to get a message through. "Danger ahead. Take it easy. Change your course. Slow down." What is your answer? Are you going to heed the signal or will you be too engrossed in the cares of this world to listen? Will you shout defiantly—as many do— "Shut up. I am busy. I'll run my own life."

The Church offers men salvation, healing, well-being in this life and for the life to come. That is guaranteed insurance because the premium has already been paid by Jesus Christ, once and for all, on the Friday we call "Good." Yet everyone is not automatically saved. Jesus died for those who consciously accept Him as their Lord and Saviour.

If they wish, people are free to choose hell instead. We are given free wills; God never forces us to join His team. We can always say, "Shut up. I am busy. I am working the Cape Race." So we live in the hell which we have made for ourselves, which we have selected as our dwelling place throughout eternity. It breaks God's heart to see us make that choice, because His Son, Jesus Christ, experienced hell Himself so that He might forewarn us. He descended into hell. Just as we will if we so choose. The difference? He rose from the dead, whereas when we make our decision it may be final.

On Good Friday, human history became divided

into B.C.—before Christ, and A.D.—Anno Domini —in the year of our Lord. When people living on the brink of disaster have once perceived the call of God, they can never again be the same. Their lives become changed into B.C.—before conversion, and A.D.—after decision. God entered history decisively on that day and offered mankind a second chance. If you were the radio operator on the *Titanic*, imagine having another chance. Would you still cable, "Shut up. I am busy. I am working the Cape Race." Or would you respond, "Thanks. Have reduced speed and changed direction. Lookouts posted."

God gave us a second chance when He sent to a world that had been ruined by selfishness and greed His Son—born uniquely but crucified commonly—to reveal the depth and tragedy of our human situation. And ever since He suffered under Pontius Pilate, was crucified, dead and buried, Christians have been saying, "Shut up. I am busy. I am working . . . for God."

3

BUT CAN WE BE MADE WHOLE?

We live in a world of brokenness: nations divided against each other, a country with warring groups each claiming racial superiority, a community broken into social classes. Families are broken by divorce, separation, or maybe just plain misunderstanding. Individuals are broken so that psychiatry reveals personalities that are split in two or even three. Brokenness, isolation, loneliness, and separation characterize our culture. What shows the isolation of man from man more clearly than a restaurant where twenty tables are individually occupied, or a train where in each double seat is one lonely soul, hungry for friendship, longing for belonging, wishing that some new passenger might sit next to him and break the "awe-ful" silence. We are not just sick, we are diseased psychologically, broken like a potter's vessel.

Yet one of man's characteristics is his "fix-it" ability. His cleverness enables him to mend broken objects. He invents a United Nations to heal the divisions between countries. He legislates to eliminate segregation. He follows the advice of the "tastemakers" who tell him what to eat, drink, wear, and smoke so that he will be exactly like everybody else—especially the important people. He moves into a new house, enrolls Sally in a new school, or seeks a new job to solve his broken family relationships. His "fix-it" ability may serve to cement some of the brokenness in the world, in his country, even in his family.

But what about the individual? What mucilage is

15

there that can heal and cement a broken personality, a sick soul? Psychiatry may be helpful, but people in this world are hurt, battered, bruised, and broken. A teenage girl is bruised from rejection by her schoolmates, a retired businessman is hurt by the callousness of his firm, a wife is damaged by the oversight of thankless children or an overbearing husband, a little boy is wounded by a relative's praise of how much smarter his sister happens to be.

Our lives are characterized by brokenness. As we get friendly with our neighbors, they move. As we enjoy our job, we get promoted. As we grow in love, we are separated by death. Life is a series of broken relationships. And our bodies have their troubles. The sportsman breaks a leg skiing, the lawyer has a coronary, the housewife learns she has high blood pressure, and the young girl develops tuberculosis. Only the rare person will pass through life without physical pain as well as emotional injury.

In the Bible we discover that the place doesn't make any difference. The sick man had been at Bethesda but was not healed. We foster the mistaken notion that people can be cured at shrines. If they have faith they may be healed at home as well as at Lourdes. We invent the crazy idea that if we move, then we will be happy. Salvation, healing, occurs in the person, not in the place.

We are told that time will bring healing. But the sick man had been waiting for thirty-eight years! Time alone does not heal. It may close the outer wound, but the inner turmoil or pain may become worse. Time can be an enemy not an ally, as ingrained habits prove. Or, when death strikes we are told that time will heal. True, but for some, time can intensify the sorrow. I know a woman with an extended grief reaction for whom time has not healed. No one on earth can heal us. Galen, the father of medicine, said, "I bind the wounds, but God heals them." Do we want to be made whole?

Jesus Christ came to heal the hurts of broken people. "He was wounded for our transgressions, He was bruised for our iniquities; the chastisement of our peace was upon Him and with His stripes we are healed" (Isa. 53:5). Jesus came to heal people like us. People with broken hopes, broken hearts, broken homes, even people with broken bones. "Today shalt thou be with me in paradise" (Luke 23:43) gave healing to the heart of a penitent thief on a wooden cross. Jesus came to heal. He healed by act, by touch, by word, by prayer.

Jesus came to bring salvation. The word "salvation" means wholeness, health, well-being, having a personality that fits together. Do we want to be made whole? If we answer Yes, then perhaps we ought to find out about the Saving Person who can put us back together, who healeth our infirmity.

Be honest! How thoroughly do we comprehend the Christian Gospel? If asked to explain it, could we? If we were asked, "Why is Jesus God?" would we have difficulty explaining? A Communist can tell us about his faith. The advertising man can tell us why his brand of cigarettes, his automobile, his toothpaste, is the best. But we Christians cannot explain the faith that is in us. We can't have the power without knowing the Person. We can't be healed by just wishing, but only by allowing Christ to come into our hearts so that we can respond in a definite act of commitment.

Imagine a boy engaged in stealing saying, "Never again. From now on Jesus Christ is my Lord and Master." Imagine a household where fighting and nastiness and viciousness occur over the dinner table saying, "Our family will start anew. God must be asked to live with us if we are to live together." And salvation will come to that house today. Imagine a man on a bed of pain knowing that the end is near saying, "Into Thy hands, O God, I commend my spirit."

When we are in a jam, when there is a fire, when a child is drowning, the cry is heard, "Save me!" In a time of crisis we need a savior. Perhaps it is a fireman, perhaps a lifeguard, perhaps a policeman, or our family doctor. In a life characterized by brokenness, tension, and turmoil, we need a Saviour. Picture a man who has fallen into a well. There he is, down a forty-foot well with smooth cement walls and with no way to get out. He cries, "Save me! Save me!"—which is exactly what God did—and does. Just when we were hopelessly lost, floundering at the bottom of the well of sin and in need of being saved, He came down. Not just with sympathy and tears, not with a book of rules, but in human form. He sent Jesus Christ down into the world, into the well of sin, to take us by the hand and lead us out.

Do we want to be made whole? Jesus Christ, and Jesus Christ alone, is the One to do the job. And the Church is the instrument which God has appointed to continue the healing work begun by His Son, Jesus Christ. The Church is a beehive, not of activity, but of worship where we gain strength to encounter a world which Christians have been commanded to claim for Jesus Christ.

The Church is a hospital where healing and salvation take place, where broken hearts are mended, where frustrated hopes are fulfilled, where men of weakness become changed into fighters for the faith. Do you want to be made whole? Are you a whole person now? Are you at war with yourself? Are you at war with others? Are you at war with God? If so, allow Christ to put you together, to give you an integrated personality in the true sense.

God has given us His Church, not as a refuge from the stress and strain of life, but as a place of healing where we can be made whole. There is only one place for broken people, for broken relationships, for broken hearts to be healed. The Church of God. There is only one Person who can effect this healing or salvation—the Man, Jesus Christ, appointed by God for this purpose. There is only one Power—the Power of the Holy Ghost, the Holy Spirit, by which God continues His saving work in the Church which He founded. And this Power is available to us.

4

WHOLE, NOT PERFECT

We usually think of good and bad, right and wrong, as two sides, forgetting that Christian doctrine considers sin as universal. We are a mixture of the saint and the sinner. Are citizens who are too busy to vote any less guilty than the politician who fakes votes? Are Northerners less responsible for racial segregation than their Carolina cousins? Are easygoing parents less responsible for mob violence than the leather-jacketed, switchblade-wielding hoodlums?

The world is not composed of two different groups of people, the good and the bad, the cops and the robbers, the virtuous and the sinful. All of us are a blend of the saint and the gangster, the villain and the hero. We are made in the image of God, with saintly possibilities, with great talent and potential, yet we mar that image with bestial passion and animal judgment. There is good even in the worst of us. Hiawatha, the Indian boy, reflects, "Even in savage bosoms there are longings, yearnings, strivings for the good they comprehend not." And St. Paul recognized that there are saints, even in Caesar's household. But One wiser than St. Paul, Jesus Christ, saw in sinful souls remarkable potential: the greedy grafter named Zacchaeus, the wanton woman at the well, the rich young ruler doomed to death by the worship of idols. Jesus sensed that their futures could be brighter than their pasts. He saw that life is a constant war between our better selves and our nasty selves. Even our virtuous acts are frequently tinged with pride and ambition, lust for power and self-aggrandizement. How often do we act in a Christian way, but for the wrong reason?

> The last temptation is the great treason:
> To do the right deed for the wrong reason.[1]

Why do we behave like angels today and like beasts tomorrow? Because we are made not just a little lower than the angels but also just a little higher than the beasts. Yet frequently our bestial nature is victorious. Don't believe it? "Connecticut boy kills parents." "Teenage girl stabbed and thrown from car." "Husband kills wife and self." "Kidnaped baby found murdered." We cannot dismiss these headlines merely by sending these people to mental hospitals or to the electric chair.

We live in a world of violence, a world that constantly tempts us to behave like beasts in a chrome-plated jungle instead of like children of God living in the vestibule of heaven. We are pressured on all sides: by our friends, "Oh, come on, don't be chicken"; by our neighbors, "So glad you like it. Why don't you buy one on time?" The temptation is for the Christian to become like the world instead of remaking the world into the family of Christ.

What are we going to do? Join a monastery or a nunnery and escape? Go along with those who would make us into a member of the blackboard jungle or a beatnik? Or cast our lot with Jesus Christ and the Church which He founded, which through the centuries has outlasted those who would have man return to his jungle practices and nature?

Are we then going to live the rest of our lives in a state of tension, frequently doing the opposite of what we know we ought to be doing?

For the conscientious non-Christian, this is an intolerable situation, to do the opposite of what he should. His conscience will not let him rest. There is no peace, only conflict and despair. The conflict cannot be resolved, for the non-Christian becomes increasingly isolated from his fellow man and separated from God. The result is psychological death or living in a state of hell, which is the end result of separation from God. If a person says, "I've been through hell," he means, "I've lived for a while without God." God has given us the Law and our conscience to reveal what we ought to do. But because of our sin, our self-centeredness, we make our choices and decisions, not from the primary desire of doing God's will but from the secondary purpose, that of fulfilling our selfish wills. There is no answer for the man caught in this situation—living apart from God. The harder he tries to do what he ought, the more he fails and the greater the conflict. As the little girl said, "The harder I try the better to be, the worser I am."

How easy to love the Jewish people who are seeking to make their home in Palestine. How easy to love the people in Asia living under such crowded conditions with meager resources. How easy to love the Negro as he struggles for equality against white opposition. Everything that is good in us tells us they are children of God regardless of race or color. But let a Jewish, a Negro or an Oriental family consider buying the house next door, and what happens? We begin to act irrationally, like beasts. Try as we will, we won't accept them as children of God, loved by Him. Indeed, we might make very sure that they didn't move in next door, and if they did, we might behave like our white cousins elsewhere by breaking their windows or igniting their houses. Within us a conflict rages between the way we *should* feel as Christians and the way we *do* feel as sinful human beings. For the conscientious non-Christian there is no resolution for this conflict.

For the Christian the good news is that God in His mercy has not left us comfortless. We have been called into a new relationship with God and, therefore, with our brother. God loved us so much that He sent His Son, Jesus Christ, here to this visited planet. Our faith in Christ makes possible reconciliation with our brother and creates a new relationship with God.

What is this relationship? That we love God and love one another. Not the sentimental love of popular songs. That's not love, and it doesn't last any longer than the tune. Nothing can make us love our neighbor; love cannot be legislated. We may like our neighbor because he is generous and loans us his boat, but when we meet the kind of person who is dirty and stupid, who clings to us like a leech, whose association with us destroys our chance of being accepted by those we want to accept us, we cannot like this person. We cannot. We don't. We hate him. Then we read the New Testament: "If any one says, 'I love God,' and hates his brother, he is a liar . . . he who loves God should love his brother also (I John 4:20-21 RSV). But we don't love our brother. There is conflict and tension. Our rationalizations allow us to go to sleep. No wonder critics say, "There are people who don't go to church who are better than some hypocrites who do."

Now find the point! Christians do not claim moral perfection. Far from it. We do not promise peace of mind if it means the absence of all conflict and tension. We do not claim to be goody-goodies. What we do claim is that we are sinners. Sinners who stand in need of God's redemption, God's saving love in Jesus Christ. We claim that life is difficult but never impossible. We confess that the decisions we make often cause us pain. We admit that we do what we ought not to do and we do not do what we should be doing. We are then sinners by confession. No doubt about it.

We who are Christians claim, however, that we are "holy people." "Called to be saints" was St. Paul's expression. Our holiness is not moral perfection, but the result of having been brought into a relationship with the Holy God, within a Holy Community; holy because it is His. Through membership by Holy Baptism in that community, we then become holy people. We are saints, and yet sinners. We face the same decisions as other men. We must make the same moral choices that others make. We will fail much of the time, as others do. What is the difference? When we have done our best, we offer it to God with love and penitence. We feel forgiven and start anew. Our anxiety is dispelled, for we know that God loves us just as we are. We are able to accept ourselves; therefore we can love and accept our neighbor, be he sinner or saint. We are delivered from viewing the world as a place with two kinds of people, the good and the bad, the sinless and the sinful, and striving to move into the perfect category. We realize that we are a blend of both and determine to make of ourselves a little more of the saint and a little less of the sinner.

5

LIVING IN A NEW DIMENSION

Conflict is not necessarily an undesirable phenomenon to be avoided at all costs; it can be creative. For the Christian the question is, How can I make conflict instrumental in growth? How can I deal with conflict fruitfully? First, stop applying value judgments and start thinking of conflict as simply the result of differences between groups or individuals, or even within a single person who has two attitudes toward the same object or person. When we acknowledge the differences that exist between people and therefore the inevitability of conflict, we are no longer upset by its appearance, we are ready to "put conflict to work." Although the mechanical engineer attempts to eliminate friction or to minimize it, he also uses it. The transmission of power by belt-drive results from the friction between belt and pulley. Friction, conflict, need not be undesirable; we can put conflict to work if we know how.

Domination and compromise are two common methods of resolving conflict. Domination disregards the sacred personality of a child of God. Our power enables us to impose our solution whether it is right or wrong. Domination never promotes growth. If a family conflict is solved by the domination of the husband over the wife or of the child over the parent, then growth is stunted. The tyrant becomes increasingly domineering and the person required to submit becomes a well-trodden doormat often committing psychological suicide. The moment when the tyrant is enjoying his position of domination could be the very moment when he is most able to foster growth in another. For the Christian, domination is not the solution.

Is compromise preferable? Most of our conflicts and differences are settled in this way. Each side acquiesces to attain peace. The teenager says, "I'll be home at 1:00 A.M." The mother says, "No, 11:00 P.M." So they agree on midnight. The union negotiator says, "Twenty cents per hour increase." Management affirms, "Not a cent." After weeks of unemployment they finally compromise at seven cents. Why didn't they in the beginning?

This highlights the weaknesses of compromise as the solution to conflict.

1. Each party resorts to extremes, certain that the more they demand the more they will achieve. The student desiring a one o'clock permission starts by asking for 3:00 A.M. The parent is uncertain of his child's true expectation, therefore may guess wrong. The result: intensified conflict.

2. Time and energy that might be spent achieving a constructive solution is expended in determining the midpoint.

3. Compromise, a temporary solution, does not create satisfaction. As soon as either party is in a stronger bargaining position—the girl has a birthday, or national security requires heavy production —restatement of the original demands can be expected.

Compromise requires sacrifice by both parties. Can Christians uncover a more desirable way of resolving conflict by which both parties can achieve their goals? An everyday example: Two girls work in an office. One prefers the window open, the other wants it closed. One opens it, the other closes it. One may resort to domination as a solution saying, "There, I've closed it and since I'm the boss, that is how it will stay." Several other solutions might be possible: lower the window from the top, put on a sweater, open the door, install a glass breakfront or air conditioning. Creative solutions to conflict may be found.

During an airline strike, a businessman was grounded in San Francisco. He was due in New York thirty hours later for an important meeting. No private planes were available. He boarded a foreign airliner, flew over the pole to Copenhagen, then boarded another plane that brought him to New York two hours before his meeting. Ten thousand miles admittedly, but a creative solution you must confess. The creative person often induces invention, whereas those with limited vision think in terms of either/or and fail to explore new alternatives. Compromise deals with things as they are, but the integrated solution requires us to put conflict and friction to work. True, a creative solution is not always possible. If Tom, Dick, and Harry all wish to marry the same young lady, there can be no resolution of their desires unless she is triplets.

The conflicts that are inevitable in life are not always with other people. Frequently we are at war within ourselves. An unresolved inner conflict can endanger our physical, as well as our mental, health. Should I work for Westinghouse or General Electric? Should I marry my home-town sweetheart or this high-fashion model? Should I buy a compact car or a convertible? Should I use this opportunity to cheat? What are my conflicts? How do I handle them? By domination? By compromise? Or, creatively?

How can a creative solution to conflict be

achieved, be it within ourselves or between persons? Frankly admit the differences instead of settling for peace at any price by denying the existence of conflict. This does not mean cessation of friendship, for Christians can differ in love. If the conflict is an inner one, admission of its existence is the first step toward salvation or healing, as Alcoholics Anonymous emphasizes. The denied conflict ferments and finds more damaging modes of expression.

When we begin to mediate, each moves toward a solution. Are we making excessive demands? Are we adhering to a position from pride while we claim we are standing on principle? What are the really significant rather than the dramatic features which divide us? Often the romantic, unlike the realist, will resort to the dramatic. The teenage boy, for example, whose parents deny him the use of the car for a date threatens, "Then I'll kill myself!" Or the irate customer says, "Cancel my charge account and send my final bill," thus resorting to the extreme. Can we perceive the significant, rather than the dramatic, ways in which we differ?

When we analyze and dissect contrasting demands, unworthy motives become evident. Piercing through the rationalizations we discover miscellaneous minor claims obscuring the true resentment. The strike mediator doubts that the relocation of the water cooler is the real reason for the workers' unhappiness. The alcoholic is forced to confess that the conflict is internal, not external.

As always, the Christian looks to Jesus Christ as an example, wondering how He resolved conflict. "Is it lawful for us to give tribute to Caesar?" they asked Him (Luke 20:22 RSV). If He answered, "Yes," the religious leaders would condemn Him.

If He answered, "No," the political figures would label Him as an insurrectionist. "Render to Caesar the things that are Caesar's, and to God the things that are God's" (Luke 20:25 RSV). He cut through the expected answer of Yes or No and added a new dimension. Whenever Christ was confronted with a conflict, He found a creative solution which people considered a miracle. As with the wine in Cana of Galilee or with the loaves and fishes on the hillside, multiplication of the limited resources occurred. Characteristic of the creative solution is this "multiplier effect" which utilizes untapped resources.

"In the world ye shall have tribulation; but be of good cheer; I have overcome the world" (John 16:33). The Christian faith acknowledges that since God made us unique individuals rather than carbon copies or in mass production, conflict exists because we were given free will. The Christian must attempt to find the creative solution, thus making conflict, like all other aspects of God's created world, serve a positive purpose.

In the New Testament, God reconciles the world unto Himself through Jesus Christ. God could have saved us from the agony of difficult decisions, eliminated conflict by making us automatons, mechanical robots. Without free will, however, we would hardly have been a worthy reflection of the Creator, in whose image we were made. God knew that this was the only way we could grow in wisdom and stature.

God could have resolved all conflict by domination; He would not utilize this method as it would not enable His children to develop. God could have compromised, enabled His Son to avoid the Cross. Compromise also would be unsatisfactory to God;

the problem of man's redemption would have been incomplete. So the Cross, the Crucifixion, was God's creative solution to the problem of evil. God was there on the Cross in Person reconciling the world unto Himself; the creative solution is not without pain and agony.

Your Lord and mine, Jesus Christ, discovered a new direction for men to look. Until He came, great leaders had tried to *push* men by force or *pull* them by the power of personality. Jesus knew that mankind needed to move in a new dimension. Gazing forward to new goals or harking backward to the time-tested landmarks was insufficient. A creative solution was needed. He sensed that men must look *upward*, and so He counseled in His last hours, "I, when I am lifted up from the earth, will draw all men to myself" (John 12:32 RSV). So He has. So He does. And so He will throughout eternity.

Conflict, strife, does not upset Christ's man— not even international strife or the end of the world, for he knows that through the Cross and the Resurrection, God has wrought for His children a creative solution.

> And there shall be signs in the sun,
> and in the moon, and in the stars;
> and upon the earth distress of nations, with perplexity;
> the sea and the waves roaring;
> Men's hearts failing them for fear . . . .
> And then shall they see the Son of man
> coming in a cloud with power and great glory.
> And when these things begin to come to pass,
> then look up, and lift up your heads;
> for your redemption draweth nigh.
>
> LUKE 21:25-28

6

GOD'S BREAKTHROUGH

Constantly we hear of scientific breakthroughs. Rare is the week when an attempt is not made to break through farther into the stratosphere. Not only is man attempting a breakthrough into God's world, God is perpetually breaking through into man's world. God breaks through in the Incarnation and stimulates the five senses He gave us. God invades the world in so many ways one cannot be unaware of His presence.

Churchmen lament that we live in a sensate culture where values and reality are based on sensory perception. But is this bad? We learn from our senses as well as from our intuition and intellect. Christians should exercise discernment in using their five senses; it would be most lamentable if Christians lacked sensitivity.

Think for a moment of your five senses: sight, sound, smell, touch, taste. Christians have X-ray vision to pierce the false, the phoney, the pretentious. Christians have high-fidelity hearing to distinguish true pitch from off-key living. Christian good taste has radically different values from that advocated by the tastemakers. Christians realize that gentleness of touch is more effective than brute force. Christians prefer things which are true, lovely and of good report, rather than the smells of shady schemes.

God breaks through and appeals to our sense of sight. This is a true experience of a twelve-year-old boy, Bob, born blind.

I walked down the path toward the woods by the school. All of a sudden a dog and another boy rushed by. They

threw a branch of a tree in front of me. I was startled and
jumped back and fell into the bushes. When I untangled
myself and got up on my feet I couldn't find the path. I
couldn't tell which direction was which. I couldn't hear
any tell-tale sounds as a guide. I called. Nobody answered.
I was surrounded by silence and confusion. After a lot of
trying and a lot of falls and scratches and bumps into the
bushes I heard the chimes of the old church. That I knew
was north of the school. I knew where I was. And I got
back all right. But that awful feeling of not knowing where
I was, which way to turn, which way to go. It was a terrible feeling. Suddenly I thought of Roy Campanella. All of
a sudden he found himself paralyzed. I asked myself would
I rather be blind like I am or would I rather be paralyzed
like Campy? And I decided the worst thing that can happen to a person isn't being blind *or* being paralyzed. The
worst thing is to lose all sense of direction in your life. And
to feel that you haven't got any place to go.[1]

Bob, like many of us, was lost in the dark; but
God—who has given most of us five senses and
Bob four—spoke through the church bell, and
Bob was saved by a sound. If God cannot appeal
to one sense He will stimulate another. God spoke
to the shepherds in a blinding flash, and He provided for wise rulers a light, a star of guidance on
their epic journey. No wonder aged Simeon could
exultantly exclaim:

> For mine eyes have seen thy salvation,
> Which thou hast prepared before the face of all people;
> A light to lighten the Gentiles,
> and the glory of thy people Israel.
>
>   LUKE 2:30-32

In time He who is the light of the world could af-
firm, "And yet show I unto you a more excellent
way" (I Cor. 12:31).

"He's blind as a bat!" Are they talking about

your lack of vision for the future, your lack of insight into yourself? "Keep your eyes open!" Is
somebody admonishing you to be on the lookout for
a star, an indication from God, an everlasting sign
that shall not be cut off?

*God breaks through and appeals to our sense of
sound.* God speaks to Elizabeth, to Mary, to Joseph,
to shepherds, to wise men, and through angel voices
to those who are attuned to the music of the
spheres. The wise men, "being warned of God in a
dream that they should not return to Herod, . . .
departed into their own country another way"
(Matt. 2:12). God may be speaking to you, telling
you to change direction. Listen! Such strange
sounds in the Bethlehem stable: the gurgling of a
child, the lowing of cattle, the heavy breathing of
tired Joseph, the rustling of the straw, and perhaps
the quiet whisper or humming of Mary, blessed
among women; plain, earthy, human sounds.

What are the revelant sounds of our day? Are
your ears so deadened with trite greetings and
cheerless cocktail chatter that you have missed
completely the simple, earthy, human noises by
which God breaks through to your sense of
sound? "You could hear a pin drop" in that stable,
in the stillness, the quiet mystery, the awesome silence in which the Almighty became human flesh.

*God breaks through and appeals to our sense of
smell.* God used frankincense and myrrh, the smell
of fresh hay, the scent of evergreen boughs. And the
Baby grown to manhood would have precious
scented balm poured lavishly upon Him by one of
His redeemed. And one day, His body would be
anointed with sweet spices for His brief descent.
These elements were used by God's agents, not
simply to mask a smell as we use deodorizers, but

to add a sense of stimulation. God has given us a sense of smell not only to enjoy His creation, but as a built-in protective device: to warn us when gas is escaping, when a fire is smoldering, when decay is present. Animals, of course, have such a highly developed sense of smell that they can discern a friend from a foe. How typical of God to allow His children of the animal kingdom, the ox and the ass, to snuggle up and smell the new Child. Not very antiseptic, but terribly compassionate.

God endows us with smell as a protective device. No person would deliberately follow the smell of poison gas or the smell of a garbage truck. Yet how many of us follow the stink and rot of low-level morality even when our sense of smell cautions us to steer clear. "I could smell it a mile away." How often have you thus referred to a shady deal, a scheme of trickery, a sharp operator. From Hamlet we gained the expression, "Something is rotten in Denmark." Macbeth refers to his murderous act, "My offense is foul; it smells to high heaven."

God breaks through and appeals to our sense of touch. Mary holding her child, the touch of her lips to the Baby's head, the earthiness, the roughness of the interior of the stable, and the penetration of the elements outside.

> In the bleak midwinter, frosty wind made moan,
> Earth stood hard as iron, water like a stone;
> Snow had fallen, snow on snow, snow on snow,
> In the bleak midwinter, long ago.[2]

How often have you said, "Keep in touch," meaning "don't lose contact"? The Incarnation assures us that God is in touch with His world, not as an absentee governor, not as a ruler emeritus; in touch because He came in a Person, Jesus Christ, to share our humanity. And since then He has remained in close contact with His children through His Holy Spirit working in the Church.

God breaks through and appeals to our sense of taste. The Christmas story is told with such delicacy and yet with candor. It hides nothing, yet is the essence of good taste. That is why the Madonna and the manger have inspired the art of the ages. What does this say to impoverished contemporary writers who wallow in filth to gain attention? God breaks through with simplicity; good taste is characterized by the simple not by the show-off, by the *core* not by the *chrome.*

"It leaves a bad taste in your mouth." How often have you thus referred not to food but to a personal encounter, a business transaction, a movie or TV program? How much of Christmas each year leaves a bad taste? How many people feel that our celebration of the Incarnation is repugnant to God and might well make the angels and shepherds vomit? The clever humorist sensed our lack of taste:

> Angels we have heard on high
> Urging us to come and buy.

God frequently breaks through into history and into people's lives. God may be trying to break through and break down the defenses we have built to keep Him out.

> He may be trying to break through your blindness to lead you by a star.

> He may be trying to break through your deafness with angel voices.

> He may be trying to break through to your sense of smell with frankincense and myrrh.

> He may be trying to break through to enable you to touch the hem of His garment.

> He may be trying to break through and endow you with a taste for the simple and beautiful.

God will break through, and unless you live in a drugged hypnotic trance, deaf, dumb and blind, He is bound to stimulate and reach at least one of your senses, as young Bob was saved by a sound. "And I decided the worst thing that can happen to a person isn't being blind *or* being paralyzed. The worst thing is to lose all sense of direction in your life. And to feel that you haven't got any place to go."

God, the great invader stealing silently into His world so that He may enter your heart and mine, breaking through our self-protecting shield, our insensitivity, and leading us to Himself. The Incarnation is thus remembered eternally as the moment of God's breakthrough, though He had been planning over the ages for this event. In time, some mysterious night or glorious morning, He will break through again to judge the quick and the dead. You and I, like the shepherds, will stand blinded by His glory, and in fear and trembling will await His words of judgment.

7

SHARING CHRIST'S CONFIDENCE

A contemporary artist depicts Jesus Christ confidently taking command of the fragile craft which the disciples feared would sink. With bold confidence Christ stands in the bow stilling the tempest, leading the ship through stormy waters. The confident Christ frequently changed the mood of his followers. Jesus, the carpenter, finds the disciples discouraged because they had fished all night without success. He steps into the boat on the Galilean lakeside and directs them when and where to cast their nets. Whereas they had caught nothing, when they follow His directions the nets overflow.

How could a carpenter, skilled with the plane and the lathe, advise a group of hardened fishermen like Andrew and Peter, James and John how and where to catch fish? It is rather presumptuous for a man of a diverse occupation to inform a specialist how to succeed; if you were to tell an engineer how to build a bridge, he might ask, "And what are your qualifications?" Yet there may be a measure of truth about life as a confident carpenter aids some distressed fishermen. The reason Christ could transform *sadness into joy, sickness into health, failure into success* was due to His confidence. We might in a given situation supply the missing link, the element of faith that inhibits technical know-how from working.

Christ had confidence *in God's plan and purpose*. The hidden Christ had existed from the beginning of eternity with the Father. He knew that God's will would prevail in history. How difficult for us to believe that good does ultimately triumph though not always on our measurable time scale. We can trace in part man's pilgrimage in history, true, but can we blueprint God's action in the future? Consider the millions of years from that moment when chaos became creation, then we realize that we are but a speck on a time chart. Yet we would use a man-made calendar or clock to measure the movements of the Timeless One.

When, like Christ, we are confident that God the Almighty is in charge of this universe, that He "calls the shots," that He has a plan for our lives, then we are delivered from wondering if life makes sense. We are freed from manipulating other people to gain our own desires or enforcing our standards on them. Paul planted, Apollos watered, but God gave the growth.

The confidence of Christ was in the master plan of His Father, our Creator! Only such certainty could have inspired Him to set His face steadfastly like a flint toward Jerusalem. When a man comes to realize that "this is my Father's world," that he is God's agent sent on a special mission, then that man can move forward with confidence, stilling the tempests, doing the work of the Father who sent and created him. Christ's confidence can be our confidence, too, when we sense that the drama on the Cross may have been for us. We realize God's will in history cannot be thwarted by scheming politicians, fearful temple authorities, cruel soldiers, or arrogant priests.

The confidence of Christ was not only in God's plan but *in human nature*. How incredible that Christ, knowing that one would betray Him, still trusted the men He had chosen. Such unimposing characters! But in spite of their inadequacy He saw in them that which others could not see: Attributes of leadership in Peter, elements of strength and loyalty in Andrew, marks of devotion and sincerity in John. And yet He perceived patterns of deceit in Judas, shadows of doubt within Thomas, and aspects of timidity in others. Still He depended upon them as He counts upon you, upon me.

He realized that many would misuse that priceless gift of God, free will, but He possessed sufficient faith in human nature not to allow the evil of a few to cancel the virtue of those who love the right. Christ had confidence in human nature. He had confidence that we, witnessing His sacrifice and that of the saints and martyrs through the ages, could see the hope of a changed humanity. Because Christ had confidence in human nature He extracted from those who followed Him their highest level of attainment. But we do not have faith in people; like Richard the Second we often lament,

> Christ . . . found truth in all but one;
> I, in twelve thousand, none.

No wonder!—because we did not perceive their God-given potential. If we have faith our Lord assures us we can move mountains, but if we have not faith then we will indeed stumble over molehills.

Jesus Christ admonished His disciples to launch out into the deep for a catch. Following Jesus Christ is a risk-taking adventure. Those who prefer to play it safe, who do not like to venture into deep waters, had better not join His adventurous band. Remember, ever remember, Jesus' phrase for those timid, spineless disciples, "O ye of little faith" (Luke 12:28). O ye of little faith, how many opportunities have been lost for lack of faith? How often

have we failed to develop the deepest in others because we assumed that human nature was frozen, in-
capable of change and growth? Jesus Christ had
confidence in human nature because man is created
in the image of God, and as a reflector of the Divine has incredible possibilities.

This is the moment when we regain our faith in
humanity, for on the Cross, the greatest human
drama ever staged, we see Jesus' unbroken confidence in men as He assures a penitent thief that he
also will meet the Father. As He forgives those who
crucified Him, He gives them the benefit of the
doubt—they did not know what they were doing.
Even after He was deceived and betrayed, pierced
and bleeding, He still expected the best from human
beings. Do you?

Jesus Christ had confidence *in Himself*. He knew
that no matter how painful the struggle, how trying the temptation, He would receive the strength
to do God's will. Some interpreted His confidence
as rudeness—when He changed water into wine
and when He assured the disciples He could feed
five thousand. But He did! On occasion we sense
His confidence wavering for a fleeting moment, but
immediately it is followed by an affirmation,
"Nevertheless, not my will, but thine, be done"
(Luke 22:42). And on the Cross His moment of
doubt is followed by His statement of trust,
"Father, into thy hands I commend my spirit"
(Luke 23:46). Jesus' confidence in Himself was
essential if He was to accomplish His divine mission. Your confidence in yourself is essential if you
are to accomplish your earthly mission.

Jesus' confidence was not cocksureness nor was
it naïveté. He knew that when we depend on God's
power our own strength and resources are multi-

plied. When God's strength is added to our own,
all things become possible. From His steadfastness
we learn self-confidence. He was the only begotten Son of God, we are merely children of the
heavenly King; yet we also, though less than perfect, bear the image of the Divine and therefore believe that God has a plan for our lives as He had a
mission for His Son. Our confidence is rewarded
as we receive strength and support during the trials
and temptations we encounter in fulfilling His plan.

Look! Jesus is passing by.
See His steadfastness—His tenacity of purpose.
Nothing can swerve Him from the road;
His eyes seem strangely set like a flint as though following
    a divine command.
Notice!
He turns His head for a moment as He travels;
He is smiling at the onlookers.
He pauses,
And with tears in His eyes but confidence in His face He
    blesses them.
Oh dear, He is passing out of sight as He rides on that
    rocky road. . . .
If You must go to Jerusalem, go the easy way,
Then they will not hurt You.
O Jesus . . . stay with us . . . do stay!
He will not listen;
That strange man persists in His purpose—steadfastly. . . .
How can He do it?
A Man cannot move to His doom with such confidence,
With such certainty,
Unless . . . unless . . .
But that could not be!
The Messiah . . . the Messiah. . . .
Then that is His secret!

Is that what He meant when He said, "I and my
Father are one" (John 10:30) and "He that hath
seen me has seen the Father" (John 14:9)?

8

THE SOURCE OF OUR JOY

"Life is not fair. Everyone else gets all the breaks. The wicked seem to prosper while the good man suffers. Can we be joyful in a world of unrest populated with selfish people?" How often have you heard it? How often have you said it? Tragically, many people do not find any joy in life. The pressures of life, the quirks of fate are just too much. These people who know no joy are in one of four groups.

1. *The existentialists* view life as having no plan, no purpose, no meaning; life goes in circles. Currently this view is expressed in "the theater of the absurd." In *No Exit* by Jean-Paul Sartre we see man trapped, condemned to a life of despair devoid of meaning. You say, "I'm no existentialist, I don't even know one." But you may practice and believe in a philosophy of life without knowing about it. If this existence is all that counts to you—with the maximum pleasure at the present moment—you may be an existentialist. "Nothingness" would be the most appropriate word to describe this view of life; life is neither good nor bad; it is simply without meaning.

> The nymphs are gone, the fairies fled
> The stars are silent overhead
> And man is left alone with man.

2. *The skeptics* have lost the joy and zest of living. They carry their skepticism to an illogical degree. No longer can they accept on blind faith what

they have been taught in church or school. This we commend; the Christian Church encourages and welcomes skeptics and doubters.

> Blind unbelief is sure to err,
>   And scan his work in vain;
> God is his own interpreter,
>   And He will make it plain.[1]

Blessings on the skeptic who wishes to doubt, provided that in time he is willing to begin *doubting his doubts* and thus achieve a sound faith suitable for maturity. The danger is that the skeptic may reject all belief, put nothing in its place, and end up an existentialist.

A college girl recently stated that she had ceased to believe in a God of judgment and could no longer be a member of a Church composed of sinful people who made so many mistakes. At the end of her lengthy explanation she was stunned when the Christian counselor replied, "I don't believe in the God you picture either, and I certainly share your feelings about the Church." The girl then realized that she was rejecting a childish belief in God and an infallible view of the Church that no mature Christian shared either; thus she replaced her "dated" views with healthy concepts.

Some skeptic is thinking, "Belief in immortality is an ancient superstition that is dying." On the contrary, history shows that man's belief in a fuller life beyond the grave in which spirit survives body is a new affirmation only a few thousand years old. Another skeptic points to a biblical passage that contradicts science or may be subject to diverse interpretations and says, "There, explain that." The answer: "My trouble with the Bible is not with pas-

sages that defy explanation, but with the passages
that are so crystal clear I cannot escape the way of
life and action they demand." Healthy skeptics and
sincere doubters are always welcome in Christ's
Holy Catholic Church. We do hope that even-
tually they will exchange *a life of doubt diversified
by faith for one of faith diversified by doubt.*

3. Even in the church are *the killjoys* who have
rejected God's created world. They lack joy in life
because they regard the world and things in it as inherently evil. Used wisely and well, God's world
is a source of joy. But when we misuse God's creation, when potash is used for explosives instead of
for fertilizer, when money is spent for garbage instead of for goods, when we kill time instead of create with it, when we waste educational opportunities for which others long, then we are poor stew-
ards indeed. When God's gifts are misused, tears,
tragedy, and joyless living inevitably follow.

The Christian regards leisure and entertainment
as part of God's created world, to be enjoyed after
the discharge of responsibilities to one's family and
one's Maker; quite essential to the happiness of a
person who finds little satisfaction in daily work.
Christians who know that this world is the secular
theater of God's glory rejoice in using God's gifts;
for them life is fun.

4. Strangely, *the pleasure hunters*, the very
people who spend their lives trying to find a good
time, lack joy and luster. This is typified in the
newspaper obituary of a man who was heir to a
multimillion-dollar fortune. The police reported
that he fell when leaving the cocktail lounge of a
plush motel, striking his head against a stone pillar.
Aged fifty, he had checked into the motel the day
before with a woman companion. He had been

married six times. In spite of his wealth, he did not find happiness in wine, women, or song. His death from a fall while leaving a cocktail lounge seemed quite symbolic of his wasted life.

Few of us may match this man. But how many of us miss true joy because we are so obsessed with our own pleasure hunt? Yet how often happiness comes, not from a deliberate search, but as a consequence of sensible living.

The inner tragedies in the lives of pleasure seekers remind one of the comic story of Billy the lizard. A salesman returned from a business trip with a chameleon for his young son, Johnny. A few days later he asked how the lizard was doing. Johnny, looking rather sad, explained, "Dad, it was this way: I had the boys in my room. Sam put Billy on my red uniform and he turned red. Mike put him on the blue camp trunk and he turned blue. Then Steve put him on the green bookcase and he turned green. Then Joe put him on the patchwork quilt and Billy bust."

How many of us are like Billy the lizard? The world we inhabit is a patchwork quilt, bewilderingly complex. We madly try to be all things to all men, to adapt ourselves to every group and environment in which we find ourselves. The outcome is "Billy bust," or in common parlance, "cracked up." Do not confuse the pursuit of happiness with the pursuit of pleasure; joy and happiness are wonderful states, but they are not synonymous with pleasure. Men of wisdom through the ages have known that happiness and joy are never found by searching, but by being. A Christian discovers that happiness is a by-product.

In contrast to these four joyless friends—the existentialist, the skeptic, the killjoy, and the pleas-

ure hunter—is the Christian who has discovered
the joy of living. He is not naïve; he does not say,
"God's in His heaven, all's right with the world."
He observes the mess that we have made. He rec-
ognizes the evil, the sordid nature of much in human
existence, but he sees beyond it.

> I know. It is not easy to explain
> Why should there be such agony to bear?
> Why should the whole wide world be full of pain?
> But then, why should her hair
> Be like sudden sunshine after rain?
>
> Turn cynic if you will. Curse God and die.
> You've ample reason for it. There's enough
> Of bitterness, God knows, to answer why,
> The road of life is rough,
> But then there is the glory of the sky.
>
> I find it ever thus. I scorn the sun.
> I con the book of years in bitter rage.
> I swear that faith in God is dead and done,
> But then I turn a page,
> And shake my sides in laughter at His fun.[2]

What is the Christian's secret? What is his source
of joy? The power of Jesus Christ! Whereas the
joyless person may admire a man named Jesus who
lived for thirty-three years, the joyful Christian believes in the eternal Christ who existed with God
from the beginning of time. Yes, He did spend
thirty-three years on this visited planet as the visible
portrait of the invisible God, but He existed with
God from the beginning of time. This is why the
Nicene Creed says, "Begotten of his Father before
all worlds," why St. John perceived that in the beginning was the Son and the Son was with God and
the Son was God.

A football coach may have a field-goal specialist

whom he saves on the bench, a player who enters
the game for the crucial moment and then returns
to the coach. So God in His infinite wisdom waited
for the opportune moment in history to send His
only created Son into the world on a special mission
of redemption. The hidden power of the hidden
Christ provides the power for joyful Christian
living and, more important, explains why Christ
was able to overcome the grave.

In a strange and mysterious way, God again
breaks through into the natural world and circum-
vents the usual process of death, as He did at birth,
so that His Son might bring good tidings of great
joy to all people. Eternal life cannot be proven any
more than one can prove that grass is green or
lemons yellow. There are many possible explanations of the Resurrection, yet the further we delve
into science the more likely becomes the possibility
that the Resurrection did occur. A noted doctor and
physicist in England have now advanced a fascinat-
ing explanation of the Resurrection based on the
theory of the acceleration of molecular velocity.[3]

For Christians the Resurrection provides the clue
whereby sadness is turned into joy. No longer need
they speculate as to whether eternal life exists.
They watch Jesus hanging next to a dying thief;
Jesus did not tell him, "I've got an idea that we
may meet again sometime after death." He said,
". . . today you will be with me in Paradise"
(Luke 23:43 rsv). Either Jesus was certain or He
was misleading the suffering man who had placed
such faith in Him. "Because I live, ye shall live also"
(John 14:19).

This same certainty led Dwight Moody, the great
evangelist, to say, "One of these days you will read
in the paper that a man named Dwight Moody of

East Northfield has died. Don't you believe a word
of it. I shall be more alive then, than I am now."
One cannot depict in detail the nature of life
everlasting; we must always resist attempts to picture it too graphically. But of the fact we are sure!
Life everlasting, eternal life, the survival of the
spirit, is not the same as immortality or being remembered in our community by our relatives and
fellow citizens.

Can we be joyful? A Christian, dedicated to
Jesus Christ and His way of life, who believes fer-
vently not only in His mission on earth but in His
triumph over the grave, has indeed a cause for joy.
He does not succumb to the despair of existential-
ism that offers no plan or purpose to existence. He
is not paralyzed by skepticism. A Christian is not a
killjoy because he believes that creation is good.
Nor is he ensnared and seduced by the pleasure
hunters who mistakenly believe that by searching
they can find the happiness and joy which can come
only through believing and being.

Can we be joyful? The Resurrection provides the
power. How else can we explain the following:
Coventry Cathedral was largely destroyed during
World War II by German bombers. The roofless
shell, however, is used for outdoor services. Above
the altar is a large cross made of a charred beam.
Carved on the wall behind the cross are two words,
FATHER FORGIVE. How easy it would have been to
have carved "Father forgive them for they know
not what they do" or perhaps even "Father forgive
them," thus perpetuating for generations to come an
attitude of blame toward the Germans.

To show that all mankind, not the enemy alone,
is responsible for the horror and bloodshed of war,
they carved FATHER FORGIVE. So this charred timber,

this empty cross, stands as a symbol in a world ready to assign blame. *Father forgive*. Never mind who is to blame. By themselves men do not have this power. It flows from the Man on the Cross, the same Man who mysteriously conquered the power of death, the Man who is to Christians the source and fountain of their life and their joy. No wonder they shout with excitement and enthusiasm, "Thanks be to God, which giveth us the victory through our Lord Jesus Christ" (I Cor. 15:57).

9

ASSURED OF OUR VICTORY

How are you and I to interpret the Resurrection? As a fairy tale? An example of wish fulfillment? An instance of miracle mongering by some Galilean peasants? Critics have intermittently tried to dismiss this central doctrine of the Christian faith as a "myth" only to discover that the Resurrection was openly referred to and universally accepted by the earliest Christians. "This Jesus hath God raised up, whereof we all are witnesses" (Acts 2:32).

One skeptic, Frank Morison, set out to disprove all existing evidence for the Resurrection. In the course of his work, he became converted to Christianity and defended the Resurrection in his book *Who Moved the Stone?*

I thought for a long time that the Resurrection was an intellectual nuisance, a belief that overstretched the credulity of a thinking man. It seemed like the happy ending which Hollywood always feels compelled to add to a story which in reality was a tragedy. I think differently now. My belief in the truth of the Christian Gospel hinges on this fact of the Resurrection. I understand why the Roman and Jewish authorities found that the really frustrating and exasperating thing about the early Christians was that they preached Jesus Christ, crucified and risen; they could not explain Him away.

The Resurrection does not mean "pie in the sky by and by when we die." The popular misconception that we are rewarded in heaven has nothing to do with the Resurrection. Nor is the immortality that poets and philosophers write about synon-

ymous with the Resurrection. Frequently immortality has been presented as the reward for believing
in immortality. In the New Testament the Resurrection provides a tremendous sense of zest, exhilaration, and triumph. Men speak of themselves as
living in a new age, as having been reborn, as having
been brought out of darkness into light, out of slavery into freedom, out of death into life. They sum
up these experiences by saying that they are living
in Christ and that Christ is living in them.

"Ye in Me, and I in you." Mystical language?
Yes, of course. But mystical language is not nonsense any more than poetical language is. It represents another dimension of human life. There are
aspects of life we just cannot explain. But are we
to be afraid of mysteries?

While we must beware of the man who is able to explain everything, we must also beware of the man who
insists on having everything explained. Our difficulties are
not in not knowing God's will for our lives—we know it
all too well—but in doing it. Our difficulties with the
Bible are not with passages we do not understand; our
difficulty lies with the passages that we understand all too
well. Passages that are so clear that we can make no mistake as to what they mean, passages that present a way of
life, thought and action that is so crystal clear I cannot
evade it. And I am not eager to do what it says. That is
my problem. Is it not yours also? [1]

The Resurrection may be difficult to understand
completely, but the power it conveys is not hard to
feel.

If we begin to see in Christ the clue to the meaning of existence, if we desire to be transformed,
then we are on the way. "If any man is in Christ, he
is a new creation, a new person." Every frozen-
food package is marked "once thawed, do not

freeze again." If, then, one's cold heart should become spiritually thawed by the warmth of Christ's Resurrection, don't put it back in the deep freeze.

He is risen! The Lord is risen indeed! Alive—on the dusty road to Emmaus, in the woodland paths traveled by St. Francis, in the devotion of John Wesley to the miners, and in the healing ministry of Albert Schweitzer. If by being alive we mean being able to walk and talk and eat, then Jesus is dead; but if by being alive we mean being in touch with people, having the power to communicate life and strength and hope, then Jesus is alive. More alive than many human vegetables who walk the streets. If *you* want to be alive as a different person, then expose yourself to the Risen Christ. The Resurrection means simply and plainly that we are sharers in, partakers of, Christ's Resurrection— here, right now, and in the world to come.

May we be clear, however, in our understanding of three points:

1. Christ died for the salvation of individuals. We often dilute the Gospel by using the phrase, "Christ died for the sins of the world." John makes clear that "God so loved the world that He gave His only Son, that *whoever believes in Him* should not perish" (John 3:16 RSV). Christ's work was performed and completed for those who accept Him and His teachings.

2. This was done *once and for all:* ". . . who made there by his one oblation of himself *once* offered. . . ."[2] That is why the Christian must avoid the position that contends one must be saved over and over again, and likewise the opposite extreme that Christ's sacrifice is re-enacted each time the Eucharist is offered.

3. This sacrifice was costly! God did not step

into history and allow His Son, Jesus Christ, to bleed on the Cross of Calvary so that a few religious sentimentalists three times in their lives could have water thrown on them, rice thrown on them, and dirt thrown on them. God is not a built-in household convenience like a thermostat to be turned on when peace of mind is needed and then turned off. I respect people who conscientiously do not have their baby baptized, who are married by a Justice of the Peace because they do not believe in the Church, or who have a private funeral without a service or a clergyman because either they or their loved one was not a Christian. Although I do not agree with them, I respect their sincerity. They don't believe in God and they don't pretend to.

Especially significant is this prophecy made by *Life* magazine:

The lackadaisical days when it didn't matter much whether you were a Christian or not may be numbered. If the recession grows stronger, you may have to declare yourself more definitely than you ever expected as to whether you believe in the Word of Christ or not. This choice, when forced on the Christian world, may be the choice that may lead to the long-awaited religious revival, a revival born in the hearts of its citizens of our time, who when forced to choose, will find no truth, no comfort, and no inspiration elsewhere.

The danger is not nuclear extermination, as graduation speakers predict. The danger is the unguided missiles of secularism, sensualism, hatred, delinquency, alcoholism, and rich living that are likely to make our society disintegrate. The issue cannot be stated too clearly.

It is: Christ or Chaos; Conviction or Compromise; Discipline or Disintegration.

Either Jesus Christ is *The Way* or He is *in the way*. There is a choice to be made. What shall we do with our lives?

Hoard them, planning everything for our advantage and advancement?

Play it safe, allowing ourselves a moderate ration of Jesus and Christian faith—just sufficient to make us think we are decent people supporting the Christian cause?

Show a vague interest in Christianity, discussing it with friends but never reaching a conclusion?

Or, follow Jesus Christ and share in His risen life?

The Gospel shows clearly what that way is. No one can say where it will lead except that it will be both difficult and rewarding. Many people will call us fools for our faith, and there will indeed be moments when we are tempted to agree.

It is a continuing struggle to hold our faith once we win it. The devil is a clever chap with many devices calculated to weaken our belief. However, in a life shared with Christ, as members of His Body, the Church, the true meaning of existence is revealed. We discover that which no suffering, hardship, not even death itself can destroy. This is the way in which we come to know Him and the power of His Resurrection.

Of all men are we most miserable if we are without hope. As a young man, Raymond Robbins perceived the truth of St. Paul's insight. He traveled to the barren Alaskan Klondike to dig gold. On his return to the coast he became lost in a blizzard. At one stage of his journey he observed two crossed pieces of white birch which marked the grave of a prospector who had fallen and been buried by the wayside. A day's aimless wandering in the storm again brought him to the same spot. He figured despondently that a lonely grave in the Alaskan wilderness was to be his fate also. Suddenly it occurred to him that not only had a man died and been buried there, but some other man, a living man, had put up the cross and gone on. What another man had done, he too could do. So he struggled through three days of blizzards until he reached a mining camp.

The greatest help we receive in perplexity comes from one who can say, "I have experienced all that." When we are in the deepest hell imaginable Jesus Christ can say, "I descended into hell also." He can assure us that although our bodies shall in God's time be put away in a wooden box, our souls are eternal. We are headed for a city which has foundations, whose builder and maker is God. "In my Father's house are many mansions; if it were not so, I would have told you" (John 14:2). He is risen! The Lord is risen indeed! You and I may share in His risen life.[3]

10

CLIMBING THE STEEP ASCENT

How mistaken our assumptions about life and religion might be. We hear: "Young people are all bad." Then what about the 97 per cent who aren't delinquents? We hear: "The Russians are all evil." Then from Tolstoy and Pasternak we gain insight, vision, and courage. We hear: "Church is for children." How about the reverse? The Christian faith is too demanding for children; it requires one on the edge of adulthood to be able to comprehend God's working in history.

Some of our ideas about God and Jesus Christ are in need of revision, too. In particular, our idea of discipleship. Many of us think we can be a disciple of Jesus in the Church and still be a playboy in the world. Contrast the current American image of "the Playboy" with the biblical picture of St. Andrew.

Andrew followed without delay. We hem and haw, trying to make up our minds about Jesus Christ. Discipleship may require that we surrender much that is dear to us: that a girl give up a boy as a marriage prospect because his idea of fun draws her from Christ; that a boy disagree with his parents about his future because they want him to take over the family business while he wants to be a doctor in the Amazon or an engineer in Liberia or a teacher in India. It may mean giving up a sports car to prepare for a Christian vocation as a social worker or a city manager or an FBI agent. Andrew didn't dilly-dally. He was man of action. He knew that sitting on the fence trying to decide never did anything but waste time and mental energy. He forsook all and followed Him.

Many of us want to have our cake and eat it too. We want to have the privilege, the glory of discipleship, the benefits of the Holy Communion, the excitement and meaning of being part of a Christian community without paying the price, without forsaking those activities and thoughts that are clearly non-Christlike: a man gambling with money, a woman gambling with her body, a young couple gambling away a life of happiness for a moment of pleasure. Andrew was an excellent follower, a better follower than a leader. We need "followers" as well as leaders. Those who will follow the Christ instead of the crowd. Andrew made his decision fast—without delay.

Andrew found Peter. He couldn't keep the good news to himself. This is the difference between a playboy and a disciple. A playboy is interested only in his own pleasure, his own prestige. He values other people only insofar as they can serve him or be used by him. He uses people instead of loving them. Andrew—what a man! He knew Peter, grew up in the same house with him, respected this powerful leader whom others admired. He realized that by asking Peter to become a disciple he was putting himself in the background. How about it? Would you invite that attractive new girl to your party? Would a young man with a shaky position in the backfield suggest to the "natural athlete" that he try out for the team?

Let the reader frankly answer these questions. Whom have you "found" since you became a disciple? Does Jesus Christ mean enough to you so that you tell people about Him? Or are you a playboy—dabbling with Christ—just using Him as a way of escaping from the house or picking up an extra date? Are you interested in your parish because it is a Christian community or because it is a place to have a good time? As a by-product you will enjoy parish life, but what is your real intent? Andrew was honest. He wouldn't use his religion as a way of making friends or dates. Disciple or playboy? If you are using people, if pleasure is your goal in life, if the Church and Jesus Christ are simply instruments, tools, then admit you are a playboy. Do not pretend you are a Christian.

Many Americans believe that the way to win customers is to buy them a drink or a lunch on the expense account, or in parishes to make converts by inviting them to a social event. Andrew wouldn't resort to this. He was direct, straightforward. He knew that discipleship which was bought wasn't worth having. It would be resold to the next highest bidder. Don't be a Christian or a disciple for the benefits you will receive. You will receive them, but they are inner, not outer. Be a disciple because you believe in Jesus Christ and His Church.

Finally, Andrew was willing to pay the price. There are many people who talk big but act small, who are keen about the plans but poor in the follow-through. "Follow-through" is an indication of maturity and discipleship. No one can count on the playboy, for at the time one needs him most he is in bed or in the barroom. He is committed to a weekend cruise or must keep an important date. His own pleasure comes first, other people come last. Andrew was different. He was no weakling; he was tough, hardened by his lakeside occupation, his hands gnarled and rough from dragging the nets and pulling the oars. He was no sissy; he was as rugged as the Cross on which his Saviour died. But he had a funny quirk about him. He didn't consider himself good enough to die on the same type of cross as his Master, so Andrew ordered his crucifiers to make a cross shaped like an X.

How much does Jesus Christ mean to us? An occasional hour when we don't have much to do anyway? A contribution if it doesn't deprive us of dancing, movies, or bowling? A few hours singing Christmas carols or working on the parish bazaar because we know we will enjoy it? Does a goodnight kiss mean more than our goodnight prayers? Does the latest issue of *Seventeen* or *Sports Illustrated* take precedence over the word of life and answer to death in God's Book, the Bible? If so, then it is rather clear who is an immature playboy and not a mature disciple, isn't it? We didn't mean it when we promised to "follow Jesus Christ as [our] Lord and Savior," did we?

Young people in the Eastern Zone of Germany climb under barbed wire fences, glide down a stream on a homemade raft to meet with Christians at a youth rally in West Germany to confess their faith in Christ, for they have little opportunity to gather in Christian fellowship in their zone. Then, after the benediction, back up the stream, bravely re-entering this zone, arriving home at dawn ready to appear in school or factory as the leaven in the lump, as courageous and contagious Christians converting Communists, piercing the iron curtain with the sword of the spirit. Only, sometimes they are caught and mysteriously disappear. Discipleship is costly. Andrew meant business. He knew a follower couldn't be a disciple *and* a playboy—he had to make a decision. Either/or.

Jesus Christ appealed so strongly to Andrew and Peter and James and John that they forsook all and followed Him. With eight other young men they remade the world. To stand for Jesus Christ and His way of life requires courage. All people do not have it, but to those who mean business He adds His strength to their own. They will discover that being a disciple is the deepest and most rewarding fun of all. The fun of the playboy is fleeting, the joy of the disciple is lasting. The pleasure of the playboy comes from using people, the delight of the disciple comes from being of service. The playboy can count on his friends only as long as he has money to treat them, until a richer playboy takes his place. The disciple can count on the love and backing of Jesus Christ down to the gates of death —and even beyond that, on His continuing Presence.

> A glorious band, the chosen few,
>   On whom the Spirit came:
> Twelve valiant saints, their hope they knew,
>   And mocked the cross and flame. . . .
> They climbed the steep ascent of heaven
>   Through peril, toil, and pain:
> O God, to us may grace be given
>   To follow in their train.[1]

11

ACKNOWLEDGING OUR DOUBLE FACE

In 1670 a London jury, after deliberation, declared a certain defendant to be "guilty of speaking aloud on Grace Church Street." The defendant was none other than William Penn, later the founder of the City of Brotherly Love.

The Society of Friends, the Quakers, of which he was a leader, had been made by Parliament an object of persecution. Penn was arrested for supposedly inciting a riotous, seditious assembly. The judges were in accord with the conspiracy against this religious minority, and the jurors were ordered to agree on a verdict of guilty and were severely threatened if they did not so find. The jurors, thank God, were outrageously impertinent and heartwarming in their response. They returned the judgment: Guilty of speaking aloud on Grace Church Street.

The judge was outraged and refused to accept the verdict. Speaking with vitriolic abuse, the judge sent them back to reconsider. These hardy jurors returned again with the same unanimous verdict, only this time in writing. "We find the defendant guilty of speaking aloud on Grace Church Street." The judge became livid and he ordered, "You will not be dismissed until we have a verdict acceptable to the Court, and you shall be locked up without meat, drink, fire and tobacco, and no one may communicate with you. We will have the verdict, or you shall starve."

On successive days the jurors returned the identical verdict. The judge became increasingly brutal and vulgar. In defiance the jury stated "Not

Guilty" and were starved for another two days. The Court finally dismissed the jury, fined them "forty marks per man and imprisonment till paid." William Penn was also jailed on a contrived "contempt of court" charge and returned to Newgate Prison.[1] Since there is no record of their release, these jurors may still be in jail nearly three hundred years later; in any instance, they exhibited amazing fortitude, immovable integrity. When men believe in a righteous cause or the innate dignity of the human being they are willing to undergo incredible hardship.

Have you ever heard or said, "He's rotten to the core"? There is deep within every person a core of inner integrity which can be uncovered through psychotherapy or revealed by Christian theology. No man is "rotten to the core." We are created in the image of God; there is implanted deep within us higher attributes of loyalty, honesty, integrity. We are also, unfortunately, inheritors of the less desirable tradition of Adam whereby we are disloyal, tricksters, corruptible. From our primeval past we have overlapped that image of God with layers of tradition to justify killing our brother or taking his land, and through our own years we have erected neat defenses in our personality structure. We rationalize our actions and believe we are altruistic when we are deeply selfish, yielding when we are domineering. We even interpret incredibly savage acts as God's Will. We guard our inner selves from being known even by our intimate friends. When we strip away our gray flannel suit many layers of undesirable covering are evident, but then we finally tap the center, the core, the true self God intended. What an amazing difference! There is the real person, there is the core of inner integrity which exists no matter how many layers of veneer. "No man is rotten to the core." This the Christian Gospel proclaims, the lives of transformed believers exhibit, and the psychotherapist affirms. No matter how rotten and false the outside layers, the core of inner integrity remains. No matter how we have defaced that "image of God" we cannot destroy it.

Falseness or rottenness is viewed as characteristic of the shady operator, noted for the sins of the flesh, but all men possess this core of inner integrity. "Many the time I have watched these prostitutes buy a meal and give money to some hopeless derelict bypassed by the social workers and the Church. They gave with no expectation of return, simply because they had human concern." So speaks a patrolman of his years on the lower East Side. The inmate of a concentration camp tells of the Nazi guard who smuggled them food and cigarettes and finally when caught was cast among them and soon put to death. No man is rotten to the core; there are saints, even in Caesar's household. There is within us that concern for our brother, that love of creation, that desire for mutual love that we have denied or buried.

Every great man in the Bible had his faults clearly pictured. Jacob deceived his brother Esau by tricking him out of his birthright, but God knew the core of inner integrity, the defaced image of God which had to be restored. Accordingly, Jacob, with his guilty conscience, had to wrestle with himself and with God so that he could again view himself in the mirror. Our Lord looked, not with judgment, but with compassion upon that woman whose behavior was regarded with disdain. "She loved much." Her mistake, He sensed, was in the unwise and random choice of the objects of her love, but He rejoiced that she knew love was important, and so His words, "Neither do I condemn thee . . ." (John 8:11).

Some people, however, develop not only personality defenses but also intellectual obstacles that prevent the reality of Christian insight from changing their lives. St. Paul was the leader of the hunt to stamp out Christians, followers of "the way." But Paul became transformed; he realized that he was not by nature given to such violent hatred. "And straightway he preached Christ in the synagogues, that he is the Son of God. But all that heard him were amazed, and said: 'Is not this he that destroyed them which called on this name in Jerusalem, and came hither for that intent?' " (Acts 9:20-21). Can we imagine the people of that day being told Saul the smiter had become Paul the preacher?

Only those willing to see themselves as they truly were, to acknowledge their shortcomings, were able to share in the growth which our Lord offered. Those certain of their righteousness, who refused to acknowledge their limitations, who saw evil in others, on them Jesus showered biting words of judgment. To the penitent He showed compassion and offered friendship; to the entrenched Pharisee He could only say, ". . . it shall be more tolerable on the day of judgment for the land of Sodom than for you" (Matt. 11:24 RSV).

"Ye shall know the truth, and the truth shall make you free" (John 8:32). This insight applies to your life, not simply to ideas in a book. The truth about yourself will make you free, will free you from the prison you have built for yourself, the protective layers you have laboriously constructed so that people will not penetrate the real you. The truth sets you free because it enables you to be open, above board, honest, the real self that God intended. At the core we have this basic integrity. You and I have the endurance of those twelve jurors to stand for the hard right against the easy wrong. We have this integrity and endurance because it is God-given.

The Christian lives under no illusion. He cannot be in accord with naïve secularists who only a generation ago believed that man was getting better and better and that the world was moving onward and upward. Nor can the Christian sink into the cellar of despair with the contemporary existentialist who sees no hope, no future, no promise, and therefore must live for the moment. Nor can he accept the position that man is hopelessly steeped in sin and sordid living. The Christian rejects viewpoints that would imply Christians are less free from the temptations and problems of the world and therefore more righteous, simply because they are Christians.

No matter how deep the sin, how numerous the layers obscuring that inner core, regardless of how the person has defaced the image of God in which he was created, the Christian knows that salvation, wholeness, healing are possible. And God may use the services of different ministers to make him well —the priest, the psychiatrist, the educator, the personnel director, the friend. Conversely, the Christian knows that no matter how exemplary the person may be at present, no matter how deep the core of integrity, he is always subject to corruption. His noble purpose may be perverted; therefore, the Christian is always on guard lest he fall. Christianity is realistic. It views man and his sin, but also glimpses God and His salvation. Christianity sees man at his *worst* and says, "Deep down is that which is worthwhile and enduring, let us uncover it." Christianity sees man at his *best* and exclaims, "There is goodness on exhibit, but quiet, the person doesn't realize it."

Theology is regarded by many as a difficult discipline to comprehend. Exercise, therefore, *imagination* rather than *intellect* and share the incredible experience of a noted scientist, writing as a poet. Loren C. Eiseley depicts the dual nature of man—man as angel, man as beast—as he travels on his strange pilgrimage in and beyond history:

Many years ago I found myself lost at evening in a rural and obscure corner of the United States. I was there because of certain curious and rare insects that the place offered. It was a country which, for equally odd and inbred reasons, was the domain of people of similar natural exuberance of character as though nature, either physically or mentally, had prepared them for odd niches in a misfit world.

As I passed down a sandy backwoods track where I hoped to obtain directions from a solitary house in the distance, I was overtaken by one of the frequent storms which blow up in that region. The sky turned dark; a splatter of rain struck the ruts of the road. Standing uncertainly I heard a sudden rumble over a low plank bridge beyond me. A man high on a great load of hay was bearing down on me through the lowering dark. I could hear through the storm his harsh cries to the horses. I stepped forward to hail him and ask directions. Perhaps, if he were generous, he would give me a lift.

There happened then, in a single instant, one of those flame-lit revelations which destroy the natural world forever and replace it with some searing inner vision which accompanies us to the end of our lives. The horses, at least at that moment, in the sound and fury of the elements appeared, even with the loaded rick, to be approaching at a gallop. The dark figure of the farmer with the reins swayed high above them in some limbo of lightning and storm.

Then, in a bolt of light that lit the man on the hayrick, the waste of sodden countryside, and what must have been my own horror-filled countenance, the rain plunged down once more. In that brief, momentary glimpse within the heart of the lightning, halved, in fact, by its wet shine, I had seen a human face of so incredible a nature as still to amaze and mystify me as to its origin. It was—and this is no exaggeration—two faces welded vertically together along the midline, like the riveted iron toys of my child-hood. One side was lumpish with swollen and inexpressibly malign excrescences; the other shone in the blue light, pale, ethereal and remote—a face marked by suffering yet se-rene and alien to that visage with which it shared this dreadful mortal frame.

As I instinctively shrank back, the great wagon leaped and rumbled on its way to vanish at what spot I knew not. As for me, I offer no explanation for my conduct. Perhaps my eyes deceived me in that flickering and grotesque dark-ness. Perhaps my mind had spent too long a day on the weird excesses of growth in horned beetles. Nevertheless, I am sure that the figure on the hayrick had raised a shield-ing hand to his own face.

One does not, in youth, arrive at the total meaning of such incidents or the deep symbolism involved in them. Only if the event has been frightening enough, a revela-tion, so to speak, out of the heavens themselves, does it come to dominate the meaning of our lives. But that I saw the double face of mankind in that instant of vision I can no longer doubt. I saw man—all of us—galloping through a torrential landscape, diseased and fungoid, with that pale half-visage of nobility and despair dwarfed but serene upon a twofold countenance. I saw the great horses with their swaying load plunge down the storm-filled track. I saw, and touched a hand to my own face.

Man passes like that swaying furious rider on the hay-rick, farther and more desperately into the night. He is galloping, this twofold creature, across the storm-filled heath of time, from the dark world of the natural toward some dawn he seeks beyond the horizon.

Across that midnight landscape he rides with his toppling burden of despair and hope, bearing with him the beast's face and the angel's dream, but unable to cast off either or to believe in either. For he is man the changeling, in whom the sense of goodness has not perished, nor an eye for some supernatural guidepost in the night. If the world were lit solely by lightning flashes, how much more we would see.[2]

Can we, like that strange rider—in part ugly and revolting, yet in part ethereal and serene—can we accept each other for what we are? Or do we expect all others to be angelic, altruistic, alluring, while we travel with our evil intent, our driving ambitions, and our secret shame? A little lower than the angels, yes, but only a little higher than the beasts.

In our family—at home or in the church—we acknowledge our achievements at our best and our failures at our worst. Here the inner core of integrity is recognized in very man. Here the fortitude and endurance of the twelve jurors is called for as each man stands by his brother, not daring to give any more serious verdict than "guilty of speaking aloud on Grace Church Street."

12

REFLECTING HIS LIGHT

A starry-eyed young couple shyly look in a jeweler's window at a diamond. Finally they pluck up courage to enter and confess blushingly that they would like to look at an engagement ring. Then the embarrassing question comes from the salesman, "What price range are you considering?" The young man, afraid of offending his beloved, is trying to say tactfully, "Not more than four hundred dollars," when that wonderful girl comes to the rescue and says, "Oh, the size or price doesn't really make any difference. I like that small one right there."

We can't tell the value of a diamond by the number of carats. Some of the largest diamonds ever discovered have been of little value because of flaws in them. Nor is the sparkle dependent upon the size or number of carats, but on three other qualities: *color*, *clarity*, and *cut*. Apply these qualities to the work of Christ's Church. A church is of value, not on the basis of the size or the number of members, but to the degree that it possesses these qualities: color, clarity, and cut.

The first quality is *color*. If a diamond were completely clear—as some imitations are—it would not be a good reflector. A certain touch of color, a bluish tint or a yellowish hue, is needed. The scientific theory of hybrid vigor, as exemplified in the multi-colored ears of corn at Thanksgiving, indicates that an attractive, appealing, colorful result ensues when we cross diverse strains.

75

Examine the color in our churches. Do we lack luster? Do we welcome primarily those who agree with us, those who come from the "right" background? How many churches are colorless, drab, cold? No wonder Mark Gibbs called his recent book *God's Frozen People*. Frequently there is more fellowship in the local saloon on Saturday evening than in many churches on Sunday morning. Could this explain why more men sit at their bars than in our pews? Does the way we welcome or reject newcomers indicate our lack of color? Consider color in its true sense! How many of our Christian neighbors of diverse background—ethnic or racial—feel compelled to travel elsewhere to "their own" church because we prefer to maintain a lily-white congregation? Are we colorful? Is our church colorful? Are we reflectors of Jesus Christ?

The second quality of a diamond is its *clarity*. When put under a magnifying glass, are there pieces of carbon that mar its perfection? When we look beneath the surface is there a vein or cleavage or flaw or split? What about the life of our churches? What lies beneath that lovely appearance: bickering? tension? gossip? What about our own lives? Could they be examined with a magnifying glass, or would we be afraid of the secret sins and hidden shame? "Almighty God, unto whom all hearts are open, all desires known, and from whom no secrets are hid. . . ."[1] Look at the flaws in human nature that mar our clarity! No person is without them. Literature reveals every man has his Achilles heel, his vulnerable spot: Hamlet, the indecisive; Macbeth, the ambitious; King Lear, the proud. No one is a perfect reflector or image of Christ Jesus and His life. Each person has a tragic flaw. What is mine? What is yours? What quality is there in our makeup which, when examined by those who know us best, leads them to say, "Don't depend on him." "She's self-centered." "He can't control his temper." "She's stubborn as a mule." These characteristics, these flaws, can become solidified in a group, so we hear of a church that is snobbish, of a church that is in a rut, of a church that is complacent, of a church that is indecisive, afraid to launch out into the deep. Do we as Christians lack clarity of voice and action on crucial issues?

The third quality that enhances the value of a diamond is the *cut*. Perhaps it is a brilliant cut, or an emerald cut. One is no better than the other, just different. Perhaps there is a lesson here: All of us are not of the same cut. How much needless tragedy and heartbreak could be avoided if we accepted this! God has molded us with a distinctness of our own, with fingertips so unique that we can be found wherever we go. Let those of us who are parents not violate that individuality by expecting a sheeplike allegiance from our children. And when we visit another church, let's try to understand their heritage and also come to appreciate our own.

The cut of the diamond in relation to a light source determines the amount of sparkle and reflection. No matter how colorful, how clear, how beautifully cut, if it is kept in the dark, we will never see its brilliance. Christ is the Light of the World; when Christians gather under the Lordship of Christ they are expected to reflect His life and teaching. "God, who at sundry times and in divers manners spake in time past unto the fathers by the prophets, Hath in these last days spoken unto us by his Son, whom he hath appointed heir of all things, by whom also He made the worlds; Who being the brightness of his Glory and the express image of his person, and upholding all things by the word of his power when he had by himself purged our sins, sat down on the right hand of the Majesty on high" (Heb. 1:1-3).

Diamonds, the songsters tell us, are a girl's best friend. For Christians, however, a diamond is a symbol of our sparkling opportunities. A diamond is hard, able to cut steel, able to shape machines. As Christians, this is our function—to be the cutting edge, the hard tool that shapes the forms and molds of society. Our Christian faith should be so colorful in its outlook, so clear in its expression, so unique in its cut that it melts the cold-hearted and pierces the hard-hearted.

In this ecumenical era we have a sparkling opportunity to make a united Christian witness, to show that cooperation has superseded competition. Christian churches need not compete with each other. What about the 38 per cent of our population who are unchurched? Only a united witness will convince them. What a sparkling opportunity to reactivate one's neighbor to full membership in his own church. What a sparkling opportunity to win for Jesus Christ and His Church that new family across the street. What a sparkling opportunity to reflect the life and teachings of Jesus Christ upon the husband and wife on the verge of separation or divorce. What a sparkling opportunity to allow the brilliance of Jesus Christ to light upon that couple in the jewelry store as He blessed the couple in Cana of Galilee. What a sparkling opportunity to bring the light of hope and the brilliance and glory of the God Eternal to an aged couple or a shut-in living in spiritual darkness. What a sparkling opportunity to allow the peace that passes understanding to infiltrate a mind twisted by mental torture.

What a sparkling opportunity? So often we lack the color properly to reflect His attractive and winning personality; so often our Church, unlike that striking warm figure of the Galilean lakeside, is colorless and cold. So often our clarity is marred by secret sins. So often our outer covering of Christian fellowship obscures a spirit of bickering and tension, unlike that of our Lord, the visible portrait of the invisible God. So often our cut is lusterless or hidden for fear of what worldly friends might say about our faith, so different from our Lord whose facets reflected so brilliantly the nature of God that people were blinded by His presence.

What difference can one person make? Let me illustrate:

About seventy-five years ago, a Philadelphia minister standing on the church steps lifted a sobbing girl in his powerful arms and inquired why her little heart was broken. "I can't go to Sunday School," she sobbed. She had been turned away, for the little church was already overcrowded with wealthy families and their children. The fatherly pastor took the child into the church and seated her in the front near him. And that day he caught a vision of the city's need. The child also received a vision. Her playmates were unable to attend; they had no place to learn the words and ways of Jesus.

Two years later, however, the little girl, who lived in a railroad tenement, died suddenly. The parents sent for the fatherly pastor to take charge of the funeral. Beneath a torn, crumpled pillow was found a soiled red pocketbook the little girl had salvaged from a city ashcan. In it were fifty-seven pennies and a note scrawled in childish hand, "This is to help build the little church bigger so more children can go to Sunday School." For two years this devoted child had run errands and placed her total earnings in the shabby purse.

When the pastor read the note and fingered the pennies he decided on action. He carried that cracked red pocketbook into his pulpit and told the story of a girl, her gift, and the grace of God. He challenged his deacons to get busy with the work of the Kingdom; he charged his adult members to consider the challenge of a little girl of the slums.

When you visit the city of Philadelphia, look at Temple Baptist Church with seats for 3,300, then Temple University with thousands of students, then Good Samaritan Hospital, and finally a Sunday-school building large enough to accommodate every child who wishes to attend. In Temple Church you will find a simple plaque in honor of Hattie May Wiatt; she was the little girl. Her beloved pastor was the famous Dr. Russell H. Conwell, author of "Acres of Diamonds," an address that raised four million dollars to make this possible. It all began with a little girl and her fifty-seven pennies from heaven that became translated into "acres of diamonds."[2]

Such were the reflectors of His word and teaching who used their sparkling opportunities. Similar opportunities confront us in our lives and in our parishes. The question is: Will we do anything about them?

13

A THREEFOLD DISCIPLESHIP

Know, Show, Go—these three one-syllable words can serve as a key to Christian life.

From our earliest years the Church tries through Christian education to nourish us with both information and experience. Knowledge is essential—to drive a car, to learn a sport, to perfect a profession. A Rotarian or a Mason knows the beliefs of his organization. A Christian needs to know, not just information but a person, Jesus Christ. Knowledge of Jesus Christ as a Person, a Power, a Force is the first step. Not knowledge *about* Jesus—when He was born, the towns where He lived, the date of His death—which any nonbeliever might know; rather *knowing* Him as a Person, as a Friend, as a Saviour.

How do we get to know Him? By studying His life; beginning and ending our day with Him. In Him we find the unique demonstration of what God is like, so that "we may evermore dwell in him, and he in us." [1]

You and I may have heard some interesting things about a person; then we spend a period of time together and say, "Now that I know him. . . ." Spend time with Jesus; look at life through His eyes. The art student looks through the eyes of his teacher, the music student listens through the ears of his teacher, the athlete observes through the motions of his coach, and the Christian, the Christian gets to know Christ by using His eyes, by viewing people and situations in the way the Master might.

A few days together rarely enables one to know a person intimately; for a Christian it takes time to know Jesus Christ. After you and He spend many hours together, sharing your joys and problems, and you find yourself asking, "What would our Lord say?" "Could I ask Him to come along?" then you are becoming fast friends. If, like Thomas, you ask, "Lord, we do not know where you are going; how can we know the way?" Jesus will answer, "I am the way, and the truth, and the life; no one comes to the Father, but by me" (John 14: 5-6 RSV).

To *know* Christ as a person, as a power, as the sharer of our life, is the key. Yet, how often do we, like Peter, deny that we are His and He is ours? "I do not know this man." "I do not know this man." "I do not know this man." (See Mark 14:68-71.) Not once but thrice Peter denied he knew Him. How many times have you denied Him for fear of what friends or family might say?

> Ashamed of Jesus! empty pride!
> I'll boast a Saviour crucified,
> And O may this my portion be,
> My Saviour not ashamed of me! [2]

Is our Saviour ashamed of us? St. Paul advised young Timothy: "I remind you to rekindle the gift of God that is within you through the laying on of my hands; for God did not give us a spirit of timidity but a spirit of power and love and self-control. Do not be ashamed then of testifying to our Lord . . . but take your share of suffering for the gospel in the power of God" (II Tim. 1:6-8 RSV).

Knowing, though essential, was not sufficient, our Lord discerned. "Wherefore by their fruits ye shall know them" (Matt. 7:20). We must *show* forth with our lives what we profess with our lips. His disciples were to show their faith at work. He did not suggest we advertise our good works; in fact, He even warned, "Do not let your left hand know what your right hand is doing" (Matt. 6:3 RSV). Being a realist, He knew we needed an example. He showed us, He demonstrated for us the way to love, the key to a Christian life, not by words but by action, not with helpful hints but with red blood. "I will show you a still more excellent way" (I Cor. 12:31 RSV). He did not talk about humility; He showed us by washing the disciples' feet. He did not talk about integration; He enacted it by mingling with publicans and sinners. He did not complain about political and ecclesiastical corruption; He drove the money changers from the temple. Critics of Christ can never say that He preached platitudes. He was a man of action: "Be ye doers of the word, and not hearers only" (James 1:22). Know Him we must, but then we are to show forth His pattern of life, His level of love, His brand of faith.

What indication is there in your life and mine that we know Jesus Christ personally and wish to demonstrate His standards? The Christian faith consists in carrying out His orders. There is a lovely legend, though only a legend, of Jesus being received again to heaven on Ascension Day. The angels welcomed Him home. One angel asked, "O Eternal Son, what plan have you made to carry on the Father's work which cost you your life blood to begin?" Jesus responded, "I have left eleven men." The angel said, "But Created One, if the eleven men fail, what other plan have you?" With confidence Jesus answered, "I have no other plan." What a magnificent faith in human nature! How "incredible" that Christ is counting on *us*. "Go therefore and make disciples of all nations . . . and lo, I am with you always, to the close of the age" (Matt. 28:19-20 RSV).

To show forth our faith we must *go* forth. With divine insight Jesus even sensed the difficulties we would encounter. "Ye also shall bear witness." Where? Jerusalem was the center, Samaria was the next ring of the circle, and finally the uttermost parts of the earth. We start with our families, then our friends; only then are we ready to become missionaries to the non-Christians in the community or world. Do we realize the implications? Jesus spoke with profundity when He ordered us to begin at home; it's easy to fool outsiders into thinking you're a Christian, but you can't fool your family or your best friends. Jesus knew this was the most trying place to witness. Until your family observe in you some semblance of His Spirit, they can say, "Practice what you preach . . . an ounce of performance is worth a pound of preaching." We need not be paragons of virtue before we can be ambassadors for Christ, for we testify not to our own goodness but to Christ's saving power. We are not the models, rather we proclaim Christ as the incomparable. Before we expect to convince our family that Christ is the wellspring of life and power, however, they should observe that we are walking in newness of life.

Jesus' amazing insight was that we are healed by *going*. "Go and show yourselves to the priests," He told the ten lepers (Luke 17:14 RSV). "Go, and do thou likewise," ended the most famous parable in history, the Good Samaritan (Luke 10:37). "Go forth in peace"; such was the Apostolic benediction.

Members of Alcoholics Anonymous realize the principle of going is essential in healing. The mission of the Christian is to go forth in His name: "Ye also shall bear witness." When do you plan to take off? First, begin in your home, Jerusalem; then with your friends, Samaria; before you serve in the uttermost parts. Discouraging at first? Of course! How few people share our Lord's wisdom that *we will not succeed in every venture:* all people may not be able to become Christians; only from time to time will we be privileged to observe success; ventures started by us are ofttimes completed by others.

Know, Show, Go. Discipleship begins by *knowing* Him, develops by *showing* Him, and is fulfilled by *going forth*.

With His courage replacing our timidity, let's demonstrate to others a higher level of life. Thus we may join the saints of the ages who were His storytellers, converting one person or sometimes a whole nation to Jesus Christ. Christians have a story to tell the nations. What a timeless tragedy if we should fail to tell it!

14

THE BATTLEFIELDS OF DECISION

What is your job as a Christian? What does Christ expect of you as His follower? I'm not about to suggest you enter the seminary or become a missionary. The testing ground of your Christian commitment will not be at the altar, in the parish hall, or in the youth center. It is not too difficult to be a Christian when surrounded by fellow Christians. The battlefields of the twentieth century where Christianity will be either saved or lost are the schoolroom, the factory, the office, the political arena, the army.

A common idea exists that to fulfill our baptismal or confirmation vows we must attend church regularly and give the clergy a helping hand. How mistaken! The test of our Christianity is from Monday to Saturday: on Monday when there is an exam on which others are cheating, on Tuesday when others leave the office early because the boss is out of town, on Wednesday when the bridge club reaches the height of malicious gossip, on Thursday when that expense account could cover a wife's birthday present, on Friday when frustration and indignation over the undeserved success of others becomes sickening, on Saturday night when sitting in a parked car. That's when the test of Christianity comes. We can't survive the test if we don't have the strength.

A faithful churchman is customarily expected to fulfill his ministry by singing in the choir, teaching church school, or by assisting the clergy. The role is actually the reverse. Rather than being the layman's task to help the clergy, it is the minister's function to assist the churchman to fulfill his ministry. Some young churchmen expect to be ministers of aviation, others ministers of education or navigation, another a minister of medical healing. Is the mechanic who services planes any less responsible for human life, any less a minister than a surgeon in the operating room? Is not the pharmacist responsible in his ministry for the proper distribution of drugs entrusted to him? Is not the engineer who builds bridges a minister, a guardian of public safety? Does not the saloonkeeper have a sacred ministry to refrain from serving those whom he knows drink excessively or squander their families' resources? Every person, then, has a ministry; and some may happen to be ordained ministers or priests as well. Then their task as ordained ministers and priests is to help *you* fulfill your Christian ministry, whether you be a schoolboy, a housewife, or a businessman. Your ministry as a Christian is to influence those with whom you work, play, and live so that they say, "Christ lives in him." "She is a follower of Jesus Christ."

A missionary from Japan tells of a convert who asked him to visit a friend in need of spiritual help on a nearby island. The request came at a time when the missionary was exhausted and he suggested that the convert take the man a Bible.

"No, teacher," replied the convert, "it is not time to take that man a Bible. Teacher, that man is reading you yet awhile. As Christ lives in you, so He will live in that man. As He fails in you, He fails in him. Teacher, as Christ lives or fails in you, so He lives or fails in a thousand homes on these islands."

That night, the missionary relates, those words kept ringing in his ears. "Teacher, as Christ lives in you, so He lives in that man. As He fails in you, He fails in him. As Christ lives or fails in you, so He lives or fails in a thousand homes on these islands."

As Christ lives in you and in me so He lives in countless thousands in the coming years. The battlefields of the twentieth century will be manned and staffed by Christians in laboratories, in offices, in unions, in country clubs, and the war for men's souls will be either gloriously won or tragically lost by us. There is work to be done; there is a world to be changed; there are people to be challenged; there are economic systems to be revised; there are outworn ideologies to be replaced; there is truth to be instilled. And Jesus Christ is counting on us.

> Creation's Lord, we give thee thanks
> That this thy world is incomplete;
> That battle calls our marshaled ranks;
> That work awaits our hands and feet;
>
> That thou has not yet finished man;
> That we are in the making still,
> As friends who share the Maker's plan,
> As sons who know the Father's will.[1]

During World War II, Christians in German concentration camps, like the early Christians, made converts by the heroic way in which they faced death. "The greatest of all trials was to remain silent and passive in the face of unimaginable wrongs. But there was one man in our camp who did not share this guilt. That was Paul Schneider, who in both word and deed protested against injustices even in the concentration camp, and for this suffered a martyr's death." [2] Could you say as you faced the firing squad for your faith, "I have only one führer, Jesus Christ"? Few of us are required to be dying examples for our faith, but all of us are expected to be living examples of it.

Sometimes, for example, a person may feel, "I'm not made of that heroic stuff. I have so little to offer Christ and His Church." Christ only asks that we offer the limited talents that we have. A twelve-year-old boy had only two small fish and five loaves, but he offered them to Jesus and they fed a multitude. An elderly widow living in a small cottage had so little—why it was only a mite—but she gave all that she had to the best that she knew and so gained immortality in heaven and in history. Jesus accepted the expensive ointment which a questionable woman poured so lavishly upon Him because He knew that this was all she had to offer that was pure and precious. A little bit goes a long way when used by God. How history has been changed by the one-and-two-talent people who have been the salt of the earth, the leaven in the lump, while erratic brilliance with its galaxy of talents has burned out unproductively!

At times the question is asked: "How can I give of myself? Is this a one-way proposition?" Christianity offers each of us the fellowship of Christ's faithful people. Because there is no such thing as a solitary Christian, one cannot be a Christian in isolation. Becoming a Christian means belonging to a fellowship that meets to gather strength, to hear His Holy Word, to receive direction in life in order to march triumphantly into the streets to confront a world that is clawing the soul of modern man to shreds.

For the Christian, life may be difficult but never impossible. Christianity does not expect us to fight this battle alone. Each of us is a member of Christ's Army, the Church, and at our baptism the hope was expressed that we might continue Christ's faithful soldiers and servants until the end of our lives. The Church provides the sacraments to strengthen us: Holy Communion to keep us close to God, Penance when we are troubled, Holy Unction when we are sick, Holy Matrimony when we are in love, and the sacraments of silence and prayer for our growth in the spirit. What Christianity does *to* each of us and *in* each of us is as significant as what it does *for* us.

Cuff was a Negro slave who lived in the South before the Civil War. He was a joyful Christian. One day his master, in need of money, sold him on the slave market. The purchaser was informed, "Cuff is a good worker, trustworthy, he has only one fault—he prays and sings all the time."

"I'll soon whip that out of him," answered the new master.

"I don't think so," said his old owner. "He would rather die than give it up."

The new master soon got word that Cuff was praying and he ordered him to stop.

"O master," said Cuff, "I love to sing and pray to Jesus, and when I pray I work all the harder."

But Cuff was sternly forbidden to sing or pray as he picked the cotton. The master heard that Cuff had been praying again, flew into a terrible rage, and had Cuff flogged. Cuff continued to work and to pray and continued to be beaten. One night his master was sorely troubled. He could not sleep. He awakened his wife.

"Shall I call a physician?" she asked.

"No," he said, "I'm afraid I'm going to hell. Is there anyone who can pray for me?"

"I don't know of anyone," she answered, "except the slave you punished this morning."

"Do you think he would pray for me," he inquired, "after what I have done to him?"

"Yes, I think he would."

The master went to Cuff's cabin and found Cuff on his knees singing:

> My suffering time will soon be o'er
> When I shall cry and weep no more.

Cuff expected to be beaten again, but his master said, "Cuff, pray for me."

"Pray for you, master? I've been praying for you all night."

At this the master dropped to his knees and, like Jacob of old, wrestled with God. The breaking of the dawn saw the breaking of a proud spirit. Master and slave embraced.

Cuff and his master later became a famous evangelistic team witnessing to the power of Jesus Christ to change men's lives.

This is what the love of God can do to even the hardest and coldest heart. Christianity takes us, breaks us, and then remakes us. It takes our iron wills and melts them in the crucible of suffering; it takes our stubborn pride and sears it with the flame of humility; it takes our self-centered adoration and pierces it with the lance that pierced His blessed side.

Each of us has been appointed an ambassador for Christ. The impression we make upon those with whom we come in contact is no less significant than that made by our ambassador to Russia or India. And this ministry may be most difficult in our own homes. One young boy said recently about his father, "I'll make a Christian out of him yet. Sis and I have him puzzled as to how Christ can make such a difference in our lives." From henceforth Jesus Christ is our leader, our constant companion, our captain in the well-fought fight. We are called to be co-workers in His Service.

Christ's servant Albert Schweitzer testified:

He comes to us as one unknown, without a name, as of old by the lakeside, He came to those who knew Him not. He speaks to us the same words, "Follow thou me," and sets us to the tasks which He has to fulfill in our time. He commands. And to those who obey Him, whether they be wise or simple, he will reveal Himself in the toils, the conflicts, the suffering which they will pass through in His fellowship and, as an ineffable mystery, they shall learn in their own experience Who He is.[3]

15

WHAT IS EXPECTED OF US?

A sixth-grade girl in a Maryland public school wrote to the editor of the *Washington Post:* "Our class is studying the world and we would like some information on the following topics: (1) how the world started; (2) how the world changed; (3) how the world actually is now; (4) our relationship to the world; (5) how we can best leave the world for those who follow." The editor replied succinctly: "I can answer just one of the questions, how the world is now. The answer is 'Terrible.' " [1]

Had the editor been writing on Good Friday after witnessing the Crucifixion, I could understand his response. Were he a convinced Christian, he could hardly be so pessimistic. A Christian who has experienced the Resurrection could provide in seven words a comprehensive answer: God requires time, expects growth, demands action.

God requires time. Gaze at a beautiful flower, a spring seed about to grow, or a newborn infant. Did they just appear from nowhere? Of course not! The wise gardener knows that the seed has been maturing in the ground, that spring flowers are not the consequence of a few April showers followed by a sunny day, but result from long, dark months of preparation, from the fertilizer spread last summer, from continual nourishment and growth. In our age, an enjoyable one which I do not condemn, we are sorely tempted to short-circuit time. We can purchase most items ready-made; it is no longer necessary to grow or prepare the vegetables, just warm them up. With a do-it-your-

95

self kit we can paint a picture by following the lines; we can make a hi-fi set by wiring the prearranged diagram. We can accelerate nearly any process. We can fly by jet to Europe, knit an afghan in moments on a textile machine, even cure with wonder drugs a disease which previously involved months of invalidism.

This is good! All of God's creation is a blessing when used properly. You and I will be able to share more rewarding and exciting experiences in our seventy years on earth than our ancestors. Some aspects of life, however, are not subject to "speed up." It still takes nine months to have a baby; it requires twenty-eight days from one moon to the next; in spite of No-Doze our bodies still demand eight hours' sleep.

Religion is in this category. There is no such thing as a prefabricated faith, a do-it-yourself kit or a bargain basement special in religion. We cannot expect on an annual shopping spree to purchase a resurrection experience, induce a rebirth of our spirit, or arrange with the bank for a new lease on life. God takes time! In the beginning God created His universe; our particular planet required six eras or ages. Over long centuries, yea millenniums, God watched His created order develop in planned progression. Then when the fullness of time was come, He sent His personal messenger, Jesus Christ, His Son, our Lord, to enable us to develop spiritually as mankind had previously grown physically. At the opportune moment in His ministry, Jesus Christ set His face like a flint toward Jerusalem; and when His hour, His time, was come on Good Friday, He commended His Spirit to His Father.

God takes time to accomplish His work. Do not expect Him suddenly to resurrect your soul without preparation on your part. God is a God of order and in His time He will enable your soul, your spirit, to grow and develop as a seed in the earth or as a child in the womb, until after a period of development and darkness you suddenly are exposed to the light and sight of creation. Religious experience is like that. If you have been living in darkness with no sense of direction or purpose, longing for the light to flood your dark path, then commit yourself for a period of time to God's nurture. As the curator, the caretaker of your soul, He will guide your growth till that day when you blossom forth and like the newborn child see for the first time the light and glory of His created world. God requires time.

God expects growth. God expects each of us to grow as a person year by year. He doesn't want us to live a humdrum, boring existence, like the man who boasted of forty years' experience in his business, to which an associate quipped, "You mean he has had one year's experience forty times." God does not expect us to grow automatically the way a youngster gains two inches a year. For our growth as persons He has given us an example. Not a statue of Buddha contemplating eternity, not a wise philosopher like Socrates, not even a warrior-king like Achilles or Caesar, but a Man on the Cross, a Man of flesh and blood. If you desire to grow in His likeness and do not fully understand Christ, place a crucifix—not an empty cross, the symbol of the Resurrection—but a crucifix on your desk or in your pocket for three days and see what happens. Or read one short book of the Bible, the Acts of the Apostles, and you may be changed.

"Isn't Christianity for sophisticated people who have time, money or a high I.Q.?" If anyone believes that God desires polish, refinement, or social status, let him look not at the Cross of Calvary, but at the cross on each side. "These men were not political prisoners nor capitalists crucified by a proletarian revolution. They were bandits plain and simple. Christ between the bandits, the Redeemer in the midst of the unredeemed, the Physician among the lepers, showing that God doesn't work through culture but through grace. He doesn't ask men to be refined; He asks them to be penitent. God reaches into the lower layers of humanity, picks out of its dregs two worthless derelicts and uses one of them to serve as the escort into paradise for His Eternal Son." [2] "*Today* you will be with me in Paradise" (Luke 23:43 rsv). No stopping off at purgatory en route; immediate salvation for Dismas, a bandit who would later become the patron saint of prisoners.

God expects growth! Yet a few people assume, "I'm already so good that I don't need it." I wonder if any of us really is as lovable as we think. Let me ask your wife about that sour disposition or that overinflated ego. A meek soul laments, "I'm much too evil to be redeemed. If God knew my past, He wouldn't even let me in the door of His House." The capacity for conversion is greater in the wicked than in the self-satisfied and complacent. Our Lord chose fiery Peter, the impulsive swordsman who sliced the ear of a high priest's slave, yet showed his love for God by dying on a cross hanging upside down. Jesus Christ never selected spineless disciples. He wanted disciples with blood and courage; blood to shed as martyrs for God's way, courage to stand before a hostile stone-throwing mob unflinchingly. That's the kind of followers He needs. People who are too big to be distracted by trivialities or miffed by pettiness. He wants all sorts and conditions of men and women. Yes, "there are many potential saints in prison and there are many potential devils in the church." [3]

Wherever you may be, whoever you are, God expects you to grow. He provides the perfect pattern so that you may grow in His stature and likeness. If you feel that you have reached the top, that no need exists for improvement, then He cannot help you. But if you recognize your need for growth, if your family is fragmenting instead of growing together, or if your ego is getting to be the size of the Empire State Building, then behold the Cross of Calvary. "Come unto me all ye that struggle and are weighted down and I will give you strength."

According to Kierkegaard, Christianity should "strip men of their disguises, compel them to see evasions for what they are, label blind alleys, cut off men's retreats, tear down the niggardly roofs they continue to build over their precious idols, isolate men from the crowd, enforce self-examination, and bring them before the Eternal."[4]

God expects growth! However, He does not expect any of us to be self-made men. He made us and offers us the pattern for perfection, but He never forces us into a decision. Like Dismas, the penitent thief, that is up to each of us.

God demands action. A friend loans you his car. You say, "Thank you." A member of your family comes to the rescue in a tight situation. You show your appreciation with a gift. A doctor pulls a loved one through a crisis and you feel deeply indebted. Parents sacrifice to send their son to college and through the years he is eternally grateful. Action demands response. God so loved that He gave His only created Son so that those who believe in Him might have everlasting life. What do you expect to do about it?

Christianity is a faith for people who are doers. Rooted in historical fact and with a firm theological foundation to support its claims, the Christian faith differs from every historical religion oriented toward contemplation and the saving of one's soul. With roots in the Hebrew tradition that stressed the "doing" of religion rather than the thinking, Christianity has accentuated this emphasis. Is it any wonder, therefore, that in less than two thousand years Christianity has accomplished more in social progress and civilization of the world than in previous recorded history? Islands of culture there had been in Greece and Egypt for a few members of the upper classes, but Christianity includes all men, slaves and emperors, soldiers and lawyers.

Beginning with Simon of Cyrene who carried Jesus' Cross, Christianity has proclaimed that all men are children of God. That particular Christians do not practice their faith is to our shame and their damnation, but the Christian faith has been unparalleled in serving as the vanguard for civilizing the world, encouraging modern medicine, fostering the climate favorable to the growth of Western capitalism, and providing for mankind the basic elements of subsistence. For twenty centuries Christians have been unmatched in their struggle to extend human progress. Now we are being challenged by the Communists, and you, yes you, will decide by your action, by your concern for the needy, whether you respond to God's act of love on the Cross. The Crucifixion was God's creative solution to the problem of evil. God could have enabled our Lord to avoid the Cross or let Him die without the Resurrection. To so compromise would have been unthinkable.

Christianity is a faith for doers, for practical people who wish to demonstrate in their lives and relationships with others the new level of life symbolized by the Resurrection. Christians are commanded to "do this in remembrance of Me" for "thus do ye show the Lord's death till He comes." Therefore, we can answer the questions of that sixth-grade girl concerning (1) How the world started; (2) How the world changed; (3) How the world actually is now; (4) Our relationship to the world; (5) How we can best leave the world for those who follow.

We can answer because we realize . . .

that God requires time: He is in less of a hurry than we are. If we are to have rebirth, a new lease on life, a resurrection, we must give God the time to work.

that God expects growth: He is disappointed when we remain either spiritual or social pygmies. He has given to us His Son, Jesus Christ, to demonstrate how we can become real persons.

that God demands action: In response to His sacrifice on the Cross we must share in His Resurrection by showing forth with our lives what we profess with our lips.

God requires time . . . expects growth . . . and demands action . . . from you!

16

RECAPTURING LOST RADIANCE

The Christian faith consists of three essential components: *thinking, feeling, acting.* From its inception Christianity has been forced to guard against individuals or groups who would minimize or distort one of these: thinking, feeling, acting.

Thinking. Christianity requires us to use the brain power God gave us. That is why Christians can never be anti-intellectual. Christianity borrowed insights from Greek philosophy and Roman poetry. Still today Christians are expected to wrestle with the problems and mysteries of life. Question! Examine! Even doubt! The Christian faith provides an answer that will satisfy us.

Feeling. Christianity claims that God endowed each of us with five senses and the ability to feel inwardly. Feeling is an essential element in human life. Without it we are insensitive, unsympathetic, unable to enjoy others or ourselves. We may reflect, "I don't trust emotion. Feeling, if not safeguarded, can run amuck, can lead you astray." True, but so can thinking. From feeling we secure the drive to act; from thinking, the direction.

Acting. In the primitive Church described in the Acts of the Apostles, doing was the natural consequence of believing. "Be ye doers of the word and not hearers only" (James 1:22). Faith without works is dead! Nineteen centuries later Christians are active as the Church is immersed in quiet works of charity and in noisy movements of protest. Think! Feel! Act! Christianity is a blend of these components. When we emphasize only one or two and ignore the third, an impoverished or distorted version of Christianity results. A three-legged stool is useless with one leg missing. So with the Christian faith if each component is not in balance or proportion.

1. If we leave out thinking, store our minds in mothballs, and emphasize only feeling and action, what happens? Without our brains to guide us, our emotions would urge the fulfillment of every impulse. In the realm of faith we would be on an emotional binge, giving free reign to every movement of the spirit, some of which might be in conflict. Without the mature reflection which thinking provides, we would be drawn into hasty courses of action. Our Christianity would become so incoherent, so illogical that new sects would emerge as history indicates. Although this picture may appear to be extreme, there are Christians who claim that thinking is not important. They even disparage a logical approach or questioning the Bible. If we do not exercise the full critical faculties of our God-given minds, Christianity will be like the three-legged stool with the first leg missing.

2. If we eliminate feeling from our faith and keep only thinking and action, what then? We would be "ivory tower thinkers" who would advocate a religious system on an intellectual basis. Feeling would not be considered a valid component of Christianity or it would be viewed as undesirable. Such "Christians" would try to know God in Christ on a rational basis and, of course, would fail. Unable to prove the existence of God, unable to secure a tape recording of Jesus' every word, they might proclaim that "God is dead."

The fundamental weakness of the "death of God" theology current in our country is that many men who proclaim it assume religion and the Christian faith is an academic exercise, subject to computer analysis or the logic of the laboratory. They do not exact such standards in every other aspect of life, e.g., in choosing a car or a wife or buying a home, but they do demand exactitude in religion.

Without the component of feeling, our action might be ineffective. A new sales manager sets forth a plan of action without gauging the feelings of his salesmen. Will it be scuttled behind his back? A government report on Medicare lists the activities which every nursing home should have and assumes that the patients have the energy of a teenager and the interests of a clubwoman. Did the author of the report ever visit a patient in a nursing home? Churches change worship and activity schedules. Have they sensed the feelings of participants? In government, in business, or in the church abortive and ineffective programs result when we forget that the people for whom the program is designed feel deeply. To ignore feeling would make our Christianity like the three-legged stool with the second leg missing.

3. The third possibility is to eliminate action and to be content with two components of Christianity, thinking and feeling. Think! Feel! But never go where the action is! In *The Brothers Karamazov,* Dostoevski describes Dmitri, "He can be carried off his feet by noble ideals . . . if they need not be paid for."[1] This was the sin of the "do-nothing" church which thought extensively, passed resolutions, felt bad about the social evils of yesterday, but either did nothing or appointed committees to do things for them, while they remained unsullied in sanctuary, monastery, or bureaucratic headquarters. If our sound thinking and deep emotions do

not lead to action, do not compel us to become deeply involved in this very world which Jesus was willing to redeem, then we have ignored the third essential component of Christianity—action. Our Christianity will then be like the three-legged stool with the third leg missing.

Thinking, feeling, acting—all are essential! Not one can be eliminated or minimized. A recent book by James A. Pike, Retired Bishop of California, sets forth viewpoints of Christ which have been held in history. As a lawyer's brief the book, *What Is This Treasure?* merits an A-plus. But it would hardly move a person or a jury to a verdict for Christ, because it assumes that the components of Christianity are primarily intellect and action, and it makes little allowance for man's emotional component. I rejoice that the author emphasizes that this treasure (the Gospel) is transmitted through earthen vessels that are made of clay and therefore imperfect. I would rejoice even more, however, if he went on to recognize that these earthen vessels who convey the Gospel are human beings with feelings. His views of Christ are presented with emotional detachment commendable for an objective presentation; but never does he consult or cite the man who knows Christ personally, intimately, on the feeling level, the man whose life has been radically changed by an encounter with "the Man for others." Such a person would testify that the view of Christ one decides to accept is not simply a matter of analysis and logic. Feeling, deep feeling, is involved.

Admittedly the "feeling" element in religion frightens many people because they have observed its misuse. They assume that a Christian witness is a lurid confession, which it is not. It is a simple testimony as to what one person feels God in Christ has meant and accomplished. This approach, as ancient as the Acts of the Apostles, is still used extensively by the advertising world. When used honestly, nothing is more persuasive. When contrived and phoney, it steels us against buying the product.

A Christian who depended solely upon feeling would certainly be as dangerous as one who depended solely upon intellect or as an action-oriented Christian whose approach ignored intelligence and feeling. Equally sick, however, would be a Christian who believed that feeling was not an essential component of Christianity. As the quiet Quaker Geoffrey Nuttall observed, "Better fanatic follies than to lie cold and unmoved in starched propriety." Hopefully, Christians will keep thinking, feeling, and acting in a healthy balance.

Christians discover as they share with others that their own faith is strengthened. Often we mistakenly assume that to be an effective witness one must be a spiritual giant. The reverse is true. A person develops spiritually as he bears witness. We bear radiant witness when we feel deeply about any issue, whether it be in politics, social affairs, or the Christian faith. Have we become so immersed in action that we have ignored the other essential component of Christianity—feeling? What do we discover on every page of the Acts of the Apostles? Radiance! As we recall the men who made Christian history, what do we find? Radiance! Where the Church is alive today, where Christ is real? Radiant witnesses! Because people have not observed that we are radiant witnesses, perhaps they have not been attracted to Christ. Perhaps some believe God is dead because His attributes have not been evident in our lives.

The radiance that emanates from a great mind, a great personality, lingers for decades. Such a person was Dr. Richard Clarke Cabot who combined a career as a medical pioneer and a professor of social ethics in Harvard University until his death in 1934. Shortly before his death he wrote an article, "Why I Am a Christian." There was not evident the reasons one expects: a Christian home, the moving sermon which converted Augustine in the Cathedral at Milan, a book read at a crucial moment; no, not even a tragic or bitter experience. Rather, he recounted the memorable day forty-five years earlier when, as a Harvard undergraduate, he listened to a visiting Scottish professor, Bible in hand, read a short passage from the fourth chapter of II Corinthians. Dr. Cabot recalls,

I saw in Henry Drummond the secret of Christianity. We faced Christ in the face of Henry Drummond that day. There was something in his face and bearing that was new to me; there was a greater combination of vigor and delicacy, of refinement and force, than I had seen before. The essential experience of Christianity is vision, confrontation, as St. Paul pictures it, in that phrase, "face to face." [2]

Richard Clarke Cabot was not ashamed to be a quiet, effective witness for Christ in his books and in his teaching. Little wonder that a professorship in his memory was established in 1966. Likewise, we are called to reflect the light of Christ so that, in a day of gloom for many, the lost radiance of the Christian faith might be recaptured. Others, seeing that life has become for us a radiant and joyful experience may be led unto Him who is the Way, the Truth, and the Life.

Think with your mind; *feel* with your heart; *act*—with your will . . . if you would set forth the Christian faith in all its fullness. All three components are essential to show that God enriches us, that Christ changes us, and that the Holy Spirit moves us into action.

17

SHOWING HIM FORTH IN OUR LIVES

The quiet, peace-loving countryside is rocked by a blast of dynamite, and a high school stands in ruins. The honeysuckle-scented air of Atlanta is sullied by the smoke from a shattered synagogue. Clinton, Rochester, Montgomery, New York, Los Angeles: we are frightened by this sudden eruption of violence in America. Until recently such violence was naïvely explained as the work of hatemongers and race fanatics. Now the attacks have broadened to include Jewish synagogues, Jehovah's Witness halls, and Roman Catholic churches. The graves of four Sunday-school girls in Birmingham make such explanations inadequate.

Why do people behave this way? Is it only because their values are threatened? Many who react in this violent manner have less to lose than citizens who support integration. Nor can we attribute this, as some do, to Communist-inspired plots to discredit America. Clever and thorough as Communists may be, this violence is indigenous, home grown. It is difficult to realize the intensity of feeling on the part of certain whites toward their brothers of a darker skin, or the intensity of prejudice among anti-Semitic people in New York, or the depth and degree of feeling that a person may possess toward one whom he despises, hates, loathes.

First, let us not equate hatred and dislike. We may dislike homework or we may find housework distasteful or we may disagree with our bosses, but this is different from hating. Hatred is an extreme emotion which frequently leads to violent action.

There is also a difference between temper and hatred. Temper is fleeting but hatred is brooding; it seethes discontent and ferments plans for revenge in the dark reaches of the soul. Think for a moment: Whom do you hate most? Have you ever felt like murder? What kept you from it? Not fear of reprisal or a jail sentence, for many perfect crimes have been committed. What restrained you from action? Even though the person seemed to merit being murdered, and the victim is not always unaccountable for his fate; nevertheless, your conscience told you that this was wrong. Perhaps you have had the privilege of a Christian heritage and influence in your life. Many have not; they are living on the moral inheritance of their ancestors. But this inheritance has been sufficiently diluted so that very little sense of innate evil remains. Might this explain some of the violence within people?

Our culture might be equally to blame. Can we, over three decades, train nearly twenty-five million men in using violent weapons and not expect a transfer to civilian life? Can we feed our children a daily diet of murder and violence on television and in magazines for fifteen years and not expect a harvest from young and old alike? Can we disregard the thousands killed and maimed yearly by automobiles and not expect to have this complacency rub off? Make no mistake! Although the price of food may have doubled in the last twenty years, the price of bodies has gone down. Human life has diminished in value. A teenage boy driving recklessly crushes a little girl against a stone wall and loses his license temporarily. Airplanes crash frequently with a hundred persons killed in a fleeting moment. Cops and robbers is played for keeps—with tragic results.

Human life is cheap. This, of course, is reflected on a national level.

Violence has become an accepted part of human life. As it erupts it becomes the duty of the state to restrain the offender by placing him in a mental hospital if emotionally sick, in a prison if a criminal, or by deprivation of his civic rights. Although we must constantly beware of becoming a police state, our courts, both local and federal, at times become so lenient that any clever lawyer can find a loophole in the method of arrest or trial or in the early childhood of the offender. Will we hear that the five men who bombed the temple in Atlanta were scared by a firecracker in early childhood and hence should be released? I do not suggest a "throw the book at them" attitude, but if those previously caught by federal and local authorities in bombings, armed robbery, and dope peddling were punished *in accordance* with the law, it might serve as a deterrent—not a cure. Individuals and groups will always test "How far can I go?" "How much can we get away with?"

Politicans use violence! Not only the corrupt political machines in our large cities, but white-collar, right-wing fascist groups have gained momentum in America. Violence is not the result of nasty men or foreign forces but an increasingly accepted part of our culture.

Consider three propositions:

1. "Hatred hurts the owner more than the victim." The victim may be permanently injured, even killed bodily, but the hater becomes infected, consumed, eaten up with this cancer so that he or she cannot think in a logical way. Everything becomes colored by this all-consuming hatred. Perhaps the

best illustration from literature is Ahab, who in his obsession to capture Moby Dick carries a whole boatload of men to their doom. A person may think that in carrying out a program of revenge he is doing God's will, that God selected him to be the instrument of vengeance. But, "Vengeance is mine, I will repay, says the Lord" (Rom. 12:19 RSV). Modern medicine observes that many measurable, physical phenomena like heartbeat, blood pressure, even blood consistency are altered by our mental state. Persons given to strong and violent feelings are more prone to heart attacks or cerebral thrombosis than those who are temperamentally "easygoing."

2. "Love is stronger than hatred." In the perspective of history, brute force may make temporary conquests but the ultimate victory is on the level of ideas. The Christian faith realizes this; secular culture does not. Who was the victor: mighty Britain with her armies ruling colonial lands, or Ghandi, the quiet ascetic man of India who demonstrated the power of nonviolence? Who was the ultimate victor: the powerful Roman ruler asking the questions, or the plain Galilean carpenter who refused to answer? Who was the victor: the Nazi guards with their fancy uniforms, or the Orthodox nun who, when she saw a young girl hysterical at having to enter the gas chamber, calmly pushed her aside and took her place? To suffer wrong is better than to inflict it. A debatable thesis? Not for Christians who outsuffered their tormenters.

3. "Hatred is contagious." The person who starts by hating one person or one group seems unable to stop there. His feelings became transferred to others. He begins by hating Negroes, then he joins the anti-Semitic bandwagon, then before long

he advocates the deportation of all aliens. He ends up at war, even with his friends. Hatred is contagious. Not only does it spread through its owner like a cancerous growth, it infects and affects every person exposed to it. It employs every technique imaginable. Slander, deceit, innuendo are the weapons. "Have you heard, the Negroes are going to buy that plot of land, then what will happen to your street?" "That's what I said, I got it from someone who knows." "It's the Jews who are making the money in the electronic field." "Sure it's true—no wonder his son hates him after doing a thing like that." Let the listener fill in the blank spaces; the rumor will be incredible by the time it travels through four people. Accusations are a favorite of the hatemongers. Watch out! Hatred is contagious. Quarantine yourself against people who have the disease.

Three questions:

1. Is hatred ever justified? We should hate sin, wrongdoing, evil. We should fight injustice whether perpetuated and perpetrated by gangsters, politicians, or churchmen. But we must hate the sin without hating the sinner. We must channel our hatred in the proper way, constructively, to eradicate the sin or evil at the very time that we are trying to love the sinner, unlovable though he may be. Perhaps you consider your hatred justifiable. A woman hated a man in her community who, while drunk, killed her daughter with his automobile. She hated him. Her task as a Christian, however, was to learn the art of forgiveness, which with God's help she was able to do.

2. Can hatred be eradicated? Although hatred will always be present in a world with sinful human beings, it need not be present in a specific person.

How can you get rid of hatred? Stop trying to prove that you have a valid reason or excuse for possessing this attitude. Face facts! For example, many still refuse to acknowledge that the blood of whites and Negroes is identical even though biochemistry proves this, and St. Paul nineteen hundred years ago said, "And God hath made of one blood all nations of men" (Acts 17:26). Some still talk of "nigger blood" or "black blood." The facts may make us realize that our hatred is founded on fancy not facts. Ask God to remove this social cancer, to free you from this wrong, bitter attitude. If you hate a particular person, exercise every opportunity to say something favorable; if it is a group, put yourself on their side of an argument. There is in every person at a given time a balance of positive and negative feelings. As soon as you allow the hostile feeling to become dominant then hatred takes over. Perhaps in a given situation you are the person to tip the scales toward love instead of hatred.

3. Is there a Christian answer? The old saying, "He who lives by the sword will perish by the sword" is equally true in the spiritual domain. He who lives on hatred will be eaten up by hatred. He who lives by the spirit will triumph by the spirit. The Bible pictures life realistically. The Old Testament contains many episodes of violence, but the New Testament demonstrates the taming of violence by the only power that is stronger—love. Our Lord says, "Do good to them that hate you, and pray for them which despitefully use you" (Matt. 5:44). "Be not overcome by evil, but overcome evil with good" (Rom. 12:21 RSV). The power of love triumphs over the love of power.

A Korean student, In Ho Oh, was brutally killed

by a gang of teenage boys in Philadelphia. For no apparent reason they jumped this innocent person whom they did not know. But there is an element of grace redeeming this act of violence, a letter from Pusan, Korea, written by In Ho Oh's parents, people with adequate cause to "hate."

To the Red Cross, Philadelphia:

Dear Sir:

We the parents of In Ho Oh, on behalf of our whole family deeply appreciate expressions of sympathy you have extended to us. In Ho had almost finished the preparation needed for the achievement of his ambition, which was to serve his people and his nation as a Christian statesman. His death leaves that ambition unfulfilled.

When we heard of his death, we could not believe the news was true, but now we find it is an undeniable fact that In Ho has been killed by a gang of boys whose souls were not saved and in whom human nature was at a standstill. We are sad now, not only because of In Ho's unachieved future, but also because of the unsaved souls and paralyzed human nature of the murderers.

We thank God that He has given us a plan whereby our sorrow is being turned into Christian purpose. It is our hope that somehow we may be instrumental in the salvation of the souls, and in giving life to the human nature of the murderers. Our family has met together and we have decided to petition that the most generous treatment possible be given to those who committed this criminal action without knowing what it would mean to him who has been sacrificed, to his family, to his friends, and to his country.

In order to give evidence of our sincere hope contained in this petition, our whole family has decided to save money to start a fund to be used for the religious, educational, vocational and social guidance of the boys when they are released. In addition, we are daring to hope that we can do something to minimize such juvenile criminal actions which are to be found, not only in your own country, but also in Korea, and we are sure, everywhere in the world.

About the burial of the physical body of him who has been sacrificed; we hope you could spare a piece of land in your country and bury it there, for your land, too, is homeland for Christians and people of democratic society, and it is our sincere hope that thus we will remember your people, and you will remember our people and that both you and we will more vitally sense an obligation for the better guidance of juvenile delinquents whose souls are unsaved, and whose human natures are paralyzed. We hope in this way to make his tomb a monument which will call attention of people to this cause. We think this is a way to give life to the dead, and to the murderers, and to keep you and us closer in Christian love and fellowship.

We are not familiar with your customs and you may find something hard to understand in what we are trying to say and do. Please interpret our hope and idea with Christian spirit and in the light of democratic principles. We have dared to express our hope with a spirit received from the Gospel of our Saviour Jesus Christ who died for our sins.

May God bless you, your people, and particularly the boys who killed our son and kinsman.

> (Signed by father, mother, two uncles, two aunts, five sisters, two brothers, and nine cousins.)[1]

Is this the quality of our forgiveness?

Was not Stephen justified in hating those who stoned him to death? Could not he have died with a curse on his lips asking God to punish them? But instead his last words echo, "Lay not this sin to their charge" (Acts 7:60). He hated the sin but not the sinner. Like his Lord, forgiveness, love, was his natural response. St. Francis of Assisi was a man much misunderstood by his contemporaries and disowned by his wealthy family, yet he prayed for them daily. And his prayer can be ours:

O Lord, our Christ, may we have thy mind and thy spirit; make us instruments of thy peace; where there is hatred, let us sow love; where there is injury, pardon;

where there is discord, union; where there is doubt, faith; where there is despair, hope; where there is darkness, light; and where there is sadness, joy.

O Divine Master, grant that we may not so much seek to be consoled as to console; to be understood as to understand; to be loved as to love; for it is in giving that we receive; it is in pardoning that we are pardoned; and it is in dying that we are born to eternal life. Amen.[2]

18

PITFALLS TO AVOID

Everything religious is presumably good. Yet many evils have been carried out in the name of religion. Like any other power, religion can be a force for good or a source of evil.

Many people use their religion as *a showpiece*, an exhibit. Unlike the Pharisees of our Lord's day, they do not wear broad phylacteries on their arms, they may not even boast about the frequency of their prayers or the extent of their giving, but for them religion is a showpiece. Since we cannot tell by their lives that they are Christ's men, they tell us with their lips how "religious" they are. Their children have never missed an attendance award, although the parents do not know the subject of the church school curriculum. There may be a plastic statue of the Blessed Virgin on the dashboard of their car—and a dancing hula girl in the rear window—and no one is sure which they worship. Religion for show! A good advertisement for business if you are a man or for your reputation if you are a woman or for your date book if you are still in school. The point is clear: Religion can be misused, can become an ornament, a showpiece, stripped of its meaning.

For others, religion has become a means of *self-interest*. "If I am religious, God should reward me." The real test of a person's faith comes in the midst of family tragedy; this is when the man of faith holds strong and the man who is misusing his religion goes to pieces. Religion for self-interest is exemplified in this prayer by John Ward, once a Member of Parliament from Weymouth, England:

O Lord, thou knowest that I have lately purchased an estate in Essex. I beseech thee to preserve the counties of Middlesex and Essex from fire and earthquakes; and as I have also a mortgage at Hertfordshire, I beg of thee also to have an eye of compassion on that county; and for the rest of the counties, thou mayest deal with them as thou art pleased. O Lord, make all my debtors good men; give a prosperous voyage and safe return to the Mermaid sloop, because I have not insured it. And because thou hast said, "The days of the wicked are but short," I trust that thou wilt not forget thy promise as I have an estate in reversion which will be mine on the death of the profligate young man, Sir John. . . . Keep my friends from sinking, preserve me from thieves and housebreakers, and make all of my servants so honest and faithful that they may always attend to my interest and never cheat me out of my property night or day.[1]

Religion a tool of self-interest! How many parents use the Ten Commandments as a club to command respect from their children instead of meriting it through godly example? In the movie *East of Eden*, the father used the Bible, not to teach God's Word, but to elicit good behavior.

Some use religion as an *escape mechanism* to avoid facing reality. How many young men enter the ministry because they would never last in a job that demanded their full energies for forty hours a week? This striking example from "Letters to Dr. Molner" in the *Providence Evening Bulletin* shows how religion can become a means of escape. Fortunately, few people misuse religion to this extent.

Dear Dr. Molner:
Our 42-year-old son "got religion" about four years ago and really has gone overboard. He refuses to take psychi-

atric treatment. He meets with his pastor hours on end in prayer, and this consecrated man says he wishes he had the faith of our son.

But there are no results—material, that is. Our son waits for the Lord to tell him what to do. Meantime, his family has gone on welfare.

What can be done for a person like this, a college graduate and a man of exceptional ability? He is soon to appear in court on a charge of non-support.

Mrs. L. J.

The answer:

This is a tragic situation, indeed. "Going overboard" in prayer and religion is not too uncommon in cases of emotional illness, nor is it surprising. While various factors may be involved, and probably are, a fundamental part of mental illness is that the individual cannot tolerate the world the way it is—or the way he thinks it is. He retires into a mental state as an escape. Often he doesn't know what he is trying to escape from, or why, but remember that this is an emotional matter, not a rational one.

Frankly, I am amazed that the "consecrated man" would take the attitude he does. It should be obvious that something is wrong with a person who spends hours in prayer and lets his family go hungry. Ministers of all faiths are, in my observation, very much alert to the problems of mental illness. As a group, they are doing great service in combating it, and I should be greatly distressed if anything I say should be taken to mean otherwise. There is no conflict between true religion and mental health. On the contrary, genuine religious faith is a bulwark of mental health.

The court appearance for non-support may be a great blessing. Perhaps someone will tell the judge what has been happening, and the court will insist on psychiatric examination.[2]

The fourth misuse of religion is more difficult to label than the first three. It might be termed *to justify one's actions.* Let me provide an example: Recently the newspapers reported that a man had shot another person. When asked by the police why he had done it, the man answered calmly, "God told me to." This man was equating his desires with God's will. And you must admit that one's desires and God's will are often rather far apart.

But many of us justify our actions by claiming that our action is God's will. Even the deeply religious person can fool himself that his actions are the carrying out of God's will when in reality one's desires might be dominant. The religious man or woman is most likely to misuse religion without realizing it, like the young girl who prayed, "O Lord, I don't want anything for myself; I just want my mother to have a nice son-in-law."

Religion can be misused: as a showpiece, as a means of self-interest, as an escape mechanism, or to justify one's actions.

But religion has a genuine use in life, too.

Instead of religion for show, there is a religion of sincerity. The word "sincere" comes from the Latin *sine cere*—without wax. Sculptors in Rome used to sell statues with cracks and imperfections which could not be noticed because they had been filled in with wax. The genuine product, the real thing without covered-up imperfections was sold "without wax"—*sine cere*. That is what religion at its best should do; not cover up the cracks and imperfections so that you are a gorgeous showpiece for the faith, but reveal your true self, without wax, sincere. "Pure religion and undefiled before God and the Father is this, to visit the fatherless and widows in their affliction, and to keep himself unspotted from the world" (James 1:27). If we are truly religious, people will know, not by show but by the radiance of our faces, the warmth of our hearts, the touch of our hands.

Instead of using religion as a tool of self-interest, it logically follows that religion, when rightly used, is the path to self-fulfillment. Notice how this paradox works: The Christian's secret is that happiness comes not by pursuit, but as a by-product of Christ's way of life. When we forget ourselves we suddenly discover that life is worth living. If religion is based on self-interest, we easily lose our faith when things go wrong. Many people who are religious for what they can get out of it become inactive when it does not guarantee that fire and flood, earthquake or tragedy will avoid their street. When religion is practiced without expectation of reward, then we find it is a means to self-fulfillment.

Rather than encouraging an escape from reality, the Christian faith confronts reality and triumphs over the sin and evil in the world. If you want realism, don't watch TV or read James Bond—that's tame. Read the Bible instead—filled with intrigue, romance, mystery, violence, but with a purpose—showing how a real, live God works to redeem a world of real people.

Anything but escape! Cain could not escape the consequences of murdering his brother; Jacob could not escape his trickery by fleeing to another country; Jonah could not escape God's assignment which sent him to Nineveh; Isaiah could not escape God's call to speak as a prophet; Peter could not escape the gaze of the Galilean which drew him from the lakeside; John the Baptist could not escape his predestined role as proclaimer of the Messiah; and Jesus could not escape the Cross if He was to fulfill the mission for which His Father sent Him.

The Christian faith does not encourage escape from reality into another world while we are still in this one. That some Christians spend their time and energy "floating on cloud 9" should not be blamed on the Christian faith. Those to blame are the persons who are afraid to confront reality with the only tool that can shape and transform it—the Christian faith. Christians do not deny suffering or tragedy, but rather use it, see beyond it, transcend it.

Finally, religion should not be misused by equating God's will with our own. Real religion provides the power to do what we do not wish to do. When we misuse religion to justify our actions, to do what we wanted to do anyway, by claiming it is God's will, we fulfill our desires and make God take the blame. Real religion provides the power to say, "I don't like doing this, but because it is God's will, I'll carry on."

Does anyone suppose that our Lord enjoyed the agony in Gethsemane and the decision to go ahead with crucifixion? Of course not! Sweat poured from His brow, the blood vessels in His arm were raised from the clenched fist, and tears filled His eyes, but He had to say, "Not my will but Thine be done." Not the resignation of a "patsy" but the decision of a man of iron will.

Accept God's will and change your life to fit it. Quite a difference from doing your will and calling God in to justify it. Here, incidentally, lies the difference between a young person who has the courage to be different from his contemporaries instead of being a carbon copy. Real religion enables you to align your will with God's, with God providing the pattern.

The Judaeo-Christian heritage is deeply aware

of the misuse of religion, the prostitution of the sacred, for prostitution is the misuse of that which is holy, sacred. Why do we misuse religion? Why do we commit idolatry? We use religion for a show-piece because each one of us has a bit of the phoney, the showoff, in him. We use religion for self-interest because we are inherently selfish, sinners who love ourselves too much. We use religion as an escape mechanism because we prefer to flee from reality rather than face and transform it. We use religion to justify our actions because we have amazing powers of self-deception; if only we can claim that God is on our side, then the person opposing us is attacking God.

Human beings will always misuse religion, but Christians, aware of this, need not. The Christian knows that although sin is inevitable in life, it is not necessary in a given situation. Genuine religion—the Christian faith at its depth—penetrates inwardly, enabling us to see ourselves as we really are, so that we are not fooled by others or by ourselves. When real religion is at work, people know it. The following story from the *New York Times* shows this.

The drafting of Roman Catholic seminarians by the Communist regime in Poland has backfired, a top army official admits.

Seminarians, on completing their service, return to the seminary—contrary to the hopes of the atheistic regime which felt that they would prefer the secular life. And when they leave the service they leave behind them a more religious army.

This admission was made by Brigadier General Bronislaw Bednarz, deputy chief for political education in the Polish Army. His report that the anti-church campaign has been an outright failure was read before a conference of army officers at party headquarters in Warsaw. He reported that only three of several hundred Catholic seminarians had rejected the religious life on completing service in the armed forces.

An alarming increase in religious sentiments had been noted in the army, inspired by the presence of the seminarians. According to observers, conscription actually provided the Catholic Church with better clerical material. Army life hardened the seminarians; they returned to training for the priesthood more mature and "better trained for life," knowing "incomparably better" the spiritual needs of men of Poland. General Bednarz also complained that units which had conscripted seminarians reported heavy increases in attendance at Sunday Mass.[3]

"By their fruits, ye shall know them" (Matt. 7:16). By the life you live, not by the words you exclaim, people will know you are Christ's man and will see in you a living mystery. In the words of Cardinal Suhard, "To be a witness does not consist of engaging in propaganda nor even in stirring people up, but in being a living mystery. It means to live in such a way that one's life would not make sense if God did not exist."

19

CHRIST, OUR ONLY MEDIATOR

We are amused when we read of South Sea primitives who worship stones, of medicine men who through incantation and sorcery try to cure sickness, of witch doctors who think they can please the gods by rain dances or sun rituals. Thank goodness we Americans of the twentieth century do not believe in magic or superstition. And yet . . .

A baby is born. The parents are thrilled. So they request, "Would you baptize Carolyn Louise on the twenty-eighth? We have friends coming from out of town and the party is all set for afterwards. Is the date okay? If anything happened to her we could never forgive ourselves if the baby had not been baptized." In other words, please wave your magic wand and sprinkle some holy water.

Four years later. "Carolyn Louise, you remember, you baptized her. Oh yes, she's grown remarkably; she has a younger brother now, guess he ought to be baptized soon. But what I'm calling about is Carolyn. She behaves terribly; my mother thought that Sunday school would teach her that commandment about obeying her father and mother." Can't the church school teachers work this magic?

Eight years elapse. "Shouldn't Carolyn be confirmed? She's twelve now, that's when I was. Can't the bishop perform this magical rite?"

Then Carolyn herself: "I want to get married to Bill. Would you wave your magic wand and make us one?"

Still later. "My husband is drinking far too much,

129

and he has started to gamble. Can you give him a talking to, he really needs it." And the minister wonders, "Shall I bring my magic wand?"

Many people do not regard their minister as any different from the medicine man of the African jungles. Their view of religion is so imbued with magic that it makes the clergy into magicians, the sacraments into mumbo jumbo, and the Church into a fortune teller's cabaret. There is still a hangover from man's dark primitive past in his desire to coerce God into helping at strategic moments in life. We do not dislike magicians, we rather enjoy them; and if someone finds a magical view of religion satisfactory, why that is just fine.

However, a magical view of religion does not explain the mysteries and tough questions of life that confront each of us: Why did my child have to die? Why has life hit me so hard? Why have my children turned out this way? Why did my wife find some other man more interesting? Why was my youthful husband taken? Why must I suffer with this terrible disease? Why can't I be around indefinitely?

There is a mystery and complexity of life unsolved by the magical view of religion. Tea leaves, palm readings, and séances will not provide an answer. How can we explain this mixture of joy and sorrow? One woman, hurt by this world, bruised and damaged by those she loved most, said, "All I want is simple happiness." The minister had to tell her that, in spite of the songsters, there is no such thing as simple happiness. In this regard the Christian is realistic about life; the secularist is naïve. Mistaken concepts of religion are common.

First, the "lifeboat" view of the Church: it's for women and children first. The weakness of this attitude is that it ignores the psychological principle that a child's view of God and authority is determined in large part by his father's attitude toward them. The child in such a situation develops a female view of God and religion. A child whose father believes in the lifeboat concept of the Church will have trouble adjusting to authority in school, in the army or in his vocation, and will think of God and the Church as a mother and not as a strong father.

Second, the "fire escape" theory of religion: it's very handy in an emergency. Which it is! Experience indicates, however, that if we are not accustomed to finding God in the likely places we will not find Him in the unlikely places when life becomes trying or tragic.

Third, the wonderful idea that we are all heading for the same place, so it does not really make any difference what god we worship, or whether we worship one. We are *not* all heading for the same place. Some people are heading for hell and at high speed. It does make a difference which god we worship because our belief determines our actions and, therefore, our behavior.

Fourth, the concept that every religion has the Golden Rule and some version of the Ten Commandments. All religions believe the same. How surprising to hear intelligent people say this! A six-week study session on what Hindus, Muslims, Buddhists, and Communists believe would quickly convince them that all religions are not alike. Contemporary as well as primitive religions show marked differences in their belief about marriage, murder, retribution, and virtue.

Fifth, every religious practice is desirable. As a little learning or the wrong kind of information can be dangerous in education, so with religion. Any force for good can be a source of evil. Religion is not a toy but an explosive power; it can excite and change people. One shouldn't play with religion; one should be in dead earnest.

If magic does not provide a satisfactory solution to the mystery of life and if popular ideas about religion are mistaken or inadequate, then what does the Christian faith have to offer? Like Churchill, nothing but blood, sweat, and tears. The blood of our Lord shed upon the Cross, the sweat of His brow as He prayed in agony and earnestness in the Garden of Gethsemane, the tears of His blessed mother at the foot of the Cross.

This world is too hard for a soft Christ, too rugged for naïve ideas of religion. No power can come to this world from a nineteenth-century picture of Christ as a sweet man who patted sheep and taught about good behavior but remained, finally, in the tomb. Only a Christ who has passed from death unto life can assure us that evil will not be victorious. Good Friday may prove that evil has its hour, but Easter affirms that God has His day. The Cross raises questions, but the Resurrection answers them. No one has to accept the Christian answers to the problems of evil, tragedy, and the mystery of life, but I challenge anyone to present a sounder solution.

The Christian faith asserts that Jesus Christ is not just a historical figure from the past. He did live and teach and suffer and die and rise again in history. The Resurrection takes us beyond tragedy through mystery to meaning. The Resurrection provides the sure and certain knowledge that we are risen with Christ. Whoever is associated with Him shares that life which is proof against death.

A little boy was frightened by lightning. His

mother went into his bedroom to comfort him. "Oh darling," she said, "don't be afraid. God is near and He will take care of us." "I know He is, Mommy, but I wish He had skin on so I could see Him." That is exactly what God did. God shared our flesh and blood and became one of us. He came down into this arena of human sin where lost men and women were away from God and made Himself real. A remarkable thing. Let this truth grip our inner minds and spirits.

> I know not how that Calvary's cross
> A world from sin could free;
> I only know its matchless love
> Has brought God's love to me.[1]

God the great reality is right here in this world with us. He came in Jesus Christ and has never left the world. We tried to throw Him out. We tried to get rid of Him. We even nailed Him to a cross. But He went on loving us, forgiving us, keeping us close to Him. And He rose again from the dead so that we might walk in newness of life. This living Christ, this God who loves, this Father who is always seeking us, is at work. He knows our problems, He can understand the weight of our crosses. He carried one Himself.

Christ is the Mediator—and a mediator is one who reconciles opposing factions, who brings people together. If you are at war with God, thinking, "Look here, God, that's enough orders from You. I'll run my own show." If you are at war with your family or, worst of all, at war with yourself, then you need a Mediator, the mediator to bring you back to God, to make you right with your family, to set you at peace with yourself.

You can take the magician. I'll take the Mediator.

20

HIDDEN POWER, HIDDEN GLORY, HIDDEN MEANING

As the atomic submarine *Nautilus* was sliding from its cradle to the ocean, Admiral Rickover was heard to remark, "I don't know why they are cheering, it's already obsolete." Life is changing at satellite speed. "Built-in obsolescence" has become a household phrase. The Christian Gospel, however, is not obsolete. Jesus Christ, the same yesterday, today, tomorrow.

The Gospel is eternal, unchanging, but the forms by which the Gospel is communicated do change. The *Revised Standard Biblical Concordance* was produced by Univac in a few hours instead of the years required heretofore for a concordance. Television provides a new medium by which God's Eternal Word may be communicated.

Three insights of the Christian faith can make life meaningful:

1. Christian faith reveals *the hidden glory* of *common things.* How easy in the chrome-plated jungle we inhabit to become entranced with gadgets and glamour while we overlook the hidden glory of common things. Ten years hence, one girl may reflect, "Those campfires and hymn sings were more fun than this night club. Those pizzas, with everyone jampacked in the church coffee house were more tasty than the caviar in this fashionable restaurant. Perhaps that wooden cross I bought for thirty-five cents with my allowance is more valuable than this diamond from Tiffany's. No, I've never yet been able to find in any encyclopedia

those gems of wisdom I gleaned from the chaplain."

Perhaps the most enduring contribution your Christian faith can provide is an appreciation of the hidden glory of common things. Not so strange for Christians who follow a Lord who talked about such everyday matters as a man sowing wheat, a builder erecting a house, or a woman losing a coin. Why, one night He took some plain bread and table wine and said, "Do this in remembrance of Me" (Luke 22:19), and He taught His followers to pray simply for their daily bread. No matter how successful we may become, let us not lose this appreciation of the hidden glory of common things. These are the "moments to remember."

2. The Christian faith reveals *the hidden power in people*. So often seemingly untalented, unpromising young men and women suddenly, under Christian influence, begin to blossom. Unrecognized talents are released, leadership potential is extracted, spiritual sensitivity is deepened. Most of us have more ability than we ever use, like the housewife being chased by a man with a butcher knife. In her frantic desire to escape, she jumped over a five-foot fence—quite an achievement we must admit. She discovered unknown resources. We, too, have untapped power. Here are the stories of two young men which testify to this hidden power in Christianity:

Jim Vaus, a wiretapper, was paid by thugs to secure information. He knew how wrong this was; he also knew the kind of men these were. Once involved, one could never get free—alive. How often information he supplied had resulted in a bullet-ridden body in a parked car. One day by accident Jim found himself in a building where Billy Graham was conducting a mission. That night Jim met

Jesus Christ. He knew he must change. As Jim prayed at home, the anxious hoodlums came after him, stood at the door with itchy fingers in their coat pockets, and asked where he had been. Suddenly, God supplied the hidden power Jim Vaus did not know existed and Jim said firmly, "I've become a Christian." The gangleader, used to handling every kind of violence or lie, was stunned this time. He didn't know how to deal with a man who quit gangland because of Jesus Christ. Perplexed, the leader walked with his henchmen back to the car and sped off. They tried to kill Jim later that week, but by then he had gone to the FBI and confessed his part.[1]

Don Maxwell, the youthful alcoholic in the movie *The Street* exclaims, "If God cared about people, there wouldn't be any Skid Row." Don found out that God did care about people, cared so much that He gave His only Son that whosoever believeth in Him should not perish but have everlasting life. What a message for Don to hear, not from a clergyman, but from a volunteer doctor binding his frostbitten feet at the Pacific Garden Mission in Chicago. Don knew that he must face the police in his hometown and, like Jacob of old, give up the alias and admit he was a robber. When the time of testing came, God stood beside Don, and so did the young telephone operator at the Mission, who had sensed the hidden power in Don.[2]

Jesus Christ released this hidden power in people. That shrewd tax agent, that impetuous fisherman, that perceptive lawyer; the very things that made them unacceptable to others made them useful to our Lord. No wonder He told them, "Follow me, and I will make you fishers of men" (Matt. 4:19). In fact, He was so convinced of the hidden power in people that He believed it took only twelve to change a world. When a group of Christians under the guidance of the Holy Spirit begin to work, the unleashed power can be immeasurable.

3. The third insight of the Christian faith which provides meaning for life is *the hidden meaning of work*. Not only is work inevitable, we discover, but enjoyable. We realize that all work is Christian.

The idea of shared work, worship, and fellowship which characterizes current Christian thinking had its twentieth-century rebirth in 1937 when George McLeod and seven others decided to rebuild the Iona Community off the coast of Scotland, which had been founded by St. Columba in 563. Now 140 of them share together; a farmer who plants the crops, a stone mason who directs the rebuilding of the ruins, a bootmaker, a cook—each man donating his particular talent to this monumental task.

One of the men, a baker, while riding on a train through England was studying his Bible, the core of Iona life. An Englishman sitting next to him said, "Oh, you're a clergyman," since he assumed only the clergy read the Bible.

"No, I'm a baker."

"Well, don't you teach Sunday school or something?"

"I'm a baker."

"Come, come, my man, surely you ought to do something for the church such as serve on the parish council or sing in the choir!"

"I'm a baker."

The hidden meaning of work! As a Christian cab driver, a Christian television producer, a Christian labor leader, a Christian on the management team, people will be looking at you. You will preach thousands of sermons every day that will either convert people to, or repel them from, Christ and His

Church. Yes, you! "No longer does the pulpit lead the world either in generating power or in initiating ideas." [3] You, as Christian bakers, Christian students, Christian bankers, Christian carpenters, are the communicators of the Christian Gospel.

"The most damaging criticism which thoughtful people make of much current religion is not that it is *untrue*, but that it is *irrelevant*. It is so tangential to life that whether it is true or not makes no real difference." [4] We try to persuade people that the Gospel is valid when their complaint is not that it is invalid or untrue, but that it is irrelevant. No religion is irrelevant if it helps people to find the hidden glory of common things they see, the hidden power in common people they know, the hidden meaning of common tasks they do. The Gospel is not obsolete, but we can prevent its transmission by failing to make it relevant.

Our Lord viewed work as cooperation with God. For many years before His thirtieth birthday, He knew how hard it was to be a carpenter. He was against the idea that men should be spoon-fed, either by the state or by their parents. He knew that men must earn their bread if they would have their bread. And the bread and wine of the Holy Communion that He sanctified on the night in which He was betrayed is representative of you, your offerings, your daily work.

The Christian faith believes in the hidden glory of common things, the hidden power in people, and the hidden meaning of work. Thus does it provide meaning for our daily lives; only thus can we be bold enough to pray:

> And here we offer and present unto thee, O Lord,
> our selves, our souls and bodies,
> to be a reasonable, holy, and living sacrifice unto thee.[5]

21

THE SACRAMENT OF FRIENDSHIP

Jesus Christ keenly discerned the distinction between a servant who has no idea what his master is doing and a friend. Between friends who share thoughts and hopes there is no superiority or condescension, but a meeting of the mind and heart.

"Henceforth I call you not servants, for the servant knoweth not what his lord doeth: but I have called you friends; for all things that I have heard of my Father I have made known unto you" (John 15:15).

Examine the nature of *true* friendship, the weakness of *false* friendship, and the basis of *eternal* friendship. How many friends does a man have? Not relatives or passing acquaintances to whom he may send Christmas cards, but persons who share his deep inner thoughts? Is not a friend that person with whom he can share common aspirations, a person with whom he labors in a life-demanding enterprise?

Friendship: the seeking and the finding by two people of the deepest in each other. Friendship is no casual encounter over a cup of coffee, no perfunctory relationship that ceases when circumstances compel a geographical separation. Friendship is not the fickle relationship of a passing summer romance. Friendship is the relationship we have with a very limited number of people whose well-being means so much to us that we suffer with them in their sorrow, we rejoice with them in their success. For a friend we will fight down to the gates of death, we will not merely give but will sacrifice.

"Greater love hath no man than this, that a man lay down his life for his friends" (John 15:13). Many depth friendships have exacted this degree of loyalty. Inconvenience, suffering, even danger do not alter the response to a plea for help from a friend. A Friend of mine thought so much of His friends that one Thursday evening He washed their dusty feet.

Is friendship desirable only from a prudential or beneficial motive, to ensure oneself attention? The Christian has a deeper motivation: "So we are ambassadors for Christ, God making His appeal through us" (II Cor. 5:20 RSV). Imagine that! We are God's messengers. So much easier to believe that God's message will come through rite and sacrament, through program and preaching, instead of through people. But it is human hearts and hands that transmit warmth and life and courage and friendship to another soul. Jesus Christ shared our humanity, not only that we might share His eternity, but so that we might transmit that humanity to others. Only as we become agents of God's love can He make His appeal for man's friendship through us.

What does friendship signify? Our friends are a certificate of character, as the amusing old camp song illustrates:

> You can tell a man that boozes,
> By the company he chooses,
> And the pig got up and slowly walked away.

The quality, not the quantity, of our friends is what counts. Their caliber is an infallible indicator of our character. Ask any credit manager! Compare your friendships with lasting friendships in the Bible:

Ruth and Naomi, a young girl and an older woman, who through bereavement and working side by side learned to share each other's hopes, joys, and tears. When Naomi returned to Judah from Moab, her widowed daughter-in-law, the Moabite Ruth, followed, saying, "Where you go I will go, and where you lodge I will lodge; your people shall be my people" (Ruth 1:16 RSV). Although separation was inevitable, their friendship endured. David and Jonathan stuck by each other through danger and adversity in spite of the fact that Jonathan's father, King Saul, tried to murder David, and David in turn on two occasions spared his life.

Our Lord found friends in every walk of life. He was even accused of being friends with publicans and sinners. And He was! He shared with Mary Magdalene penitence for her past and hope for her future. He was older brother and companion to John the Beloved. He wept at the grave of Lazarus, His friend. Even the least brilliant He regarded as friends, not servants.

What will biographers record about each of us? Will it be said proudly: "The gossiping Roman annalist, who found specks on every other sun, never suggested scandal or criticism about his public or private life. Agrippa, the noblest Roman of his day, is the chief instance in history of a man of first-class talents who was content to subordinate them to the interests of a friend." [1]

A century ago, Nathaniel Hawthorne dedicated a book to his old friend Franklin Pierce, by then in disrepute. Hawthorne's publishers advised that to do so would hurt sales of the book. Hawthorne responded, "I cannot withdraw the dedication. If he is so unpopular that his name is enough to sink the volume, there is so much the more need that an old friend should stand by him. I cannot, merely on account of profit or reputation, go back from what I felt right to do, and if I were to tear out the dedication I should never look at the volume again without remorse and shame." [2]

Nearer to our own day, a man who felt sufficiently indebted to President Lowell of Harvard to leave a large sum of money in his memory stated, "He proved to me for twenty-five years a most delightful friend for he kept up a constant supply of what was most needed—sympathy and encouragement." [3]

Contemporary examples still confront us. In years to come will friends reflect: "He was a true friend through thick and thin." Or will they say: "For many years we were close friends; but after he achieved success and wealth he never returned to the scene of his birth or acknowledged that we existed."

True friendship endures. How naïve if we did not recognize that many "friendships" prove to be false. Job berates his friends, "You are empty streams, a disappearing mirage. Men come to you harassed and beset, find nothing and then turn away" (Job 6:15-18, adapted). Job, like the poet, sensed false friendship.

> Last night, O friend of mine, unto your door
> With wearied soul and heart most sore,
> I came to cry for comfort. And you
> Gave me light words, light praise, your jester's due:
> I shall not come for comfort any more.
>
> Take you my laughter, since you love it so.
> The little jests men juggle to and fro.
> I did not guess how much I came to ask,
> I did not guess how difficult the task
> Your solace for a heart you did not know.[4]

False friendship—how tragic when what was conceived to be an enduring relationship is ruptured. Does this poem about Roland, the French literary hero, apply to a friendship that once existed for you?

> Alas! they had been friends in youth;
> But whispering tongues can poison truth;
> And constancy lives in realms above;
> And life is thorny; and youth is vain;
> And to be wroth with one we love
> Doth work like madness in the brain.
> And thus it chanced, as I divine,
> With Roland and Sir Leoline.
> Each spake words of high disdain
> And insult to his heart's best brother:
> They parted—ne'er to meet again!
> But never either found another
> To free the hollow heart from paining—
> They stood aloof, the scars remaining,
> Like cliffs which had been rent asunder;
> A dreary sea now flows between.
> But neither heat, nor frost, nor thunder,
> Shall wholly do away, I we'en,
> The marks of that which once hath been.[5]

Although true friendship may never be erased it can be irreparably damaged in many ways:

When one party gives credence to an outsider's nasty rumors, distrust enters, and intimacy departs.

When one offers the other only the dregs of his time, his talent, and his energy.

When one develops a compulsive need for exclusive possession of the other's affection or time, and cannot permit his friend to have another friend.

When one friend tips the delicate balance of equality by assuming a view of condescension.

There is in our era a danger that true friendship will be misunderstood by nearsighted psychologists and amateur psychiatrists who explain away depth relationships with the jargon of their cult: father figure, mother figure, dependency relationship, latent homosexuality. Thus they would explain the classic friendships of history.

We cannot in such cavalier fashion penetrate the deep recesses of the human heart. In the book *In Search of Maturity*, Fritz Kunkel expresses it: "The autobiography of a man like St. Augustine is to men like Freud and Adler what a painting by Raphael would be to a blind man." [6] There are depths and dimensions of human devotion that defy dissection. Do we then dare deface the friendships of others by labels and categories?

Even with true friends, however, the moment of parting in this world may come.

> When we at death must part,
> Not like the world's, our pain;
> But one in Christ, and one in heart,
> We part to meet again.[7]

Our friendship may diminish with time and distance. Imagine having a friend who promises, "I will never leave thee nor forsake thee." That's what my Friend has promised me. Because earthly friendships are severed by death, because we live in a world where false friendships may scar our souls and pierce our hearts, we need eternal friendship that transcends time and place. Human friendship is wonderful, but eternal friendship is glorious, for "None of us lives to himself, and none of us dies to himself . . . whether we live or whether we die, we are the Lord's" (Rom. 14:7-8 RSV).

Christians stand in a relationship to Jesus Christ which makes them not servants but friends. Not a onesided relationship but a love affair where each gives to the other.

We offer weakness. He returns strength.

We offer our scarlet sins. He returns them whiter than snow.

We bring bread and wine. He provides the Supper of the Lord.

We offer shattered hopes. He offers a balm in Gilead to heal the sin-sick soul.

That's the quality of the friendship Christ offers —Eternal Friendship. Not for "as long as we both shall live" but eternally. Because He shared our humanity, we share His eternity. How do I know? He said so. "In my Father's house are many mansions: if it were not so I would have told you. I go to prepare a place for you . . . that where I am, there ye may be also" (John 14:2-3). We can believe Him, for Jesus Christ does not lie or deceive. Family may fail us, friends desert us, but He it is who is with us.

> In our joys and in our sorrows,
>   Days of toil and hours of ease,
> Still He calls, in cares and pleasures,
>   "Christian love me more than these." [8]

He who first loved us when we were most unlovable and unlovely has honored us by calling us, not servants who know not what the master doeth, but friends. For all things which He has heard of the Father He has made known unto us. Greater love hath no man than this that He lay down his life for His friends—on the Cross of Calvary.

NOTES

Although the following notes acknowledge specific references, an author can never properly assign credit for the ideas and illustrations garnered over the years from teachers and colleagues. Special acknowledgment is due, however, to four talented communicators of the Christian faith: the late G. A. Studdert-Kennedy, the late Peter Marshall, Canon Bryan Green, and the Right Reverend Fulton J. Sheen. One cannot read their works without being influenced by their manner of presentation.

FOR CHAPTER 1: *Niagara Moments*

[1] "The Night Niagara Stopped," *Natural History* (Sept., 1956), pp. 362-363.

FOR CHAPTER 4: *Whole, Not Perfect*

[1] T. S. Eliot, "Murder in the Cathedral," Part 1, *The Complete Poems and Plays of T. S. Eliot* (New York: Harcourt, Brace & World, 1952).

FOR CHAPTER 6: *God's Breakthrough*

[1] Howard A. Rusk, "Light in Darkness," *The Laymen's Movement Review*, Jan.-Feb., 1959. [2] Christina Rossetti, *The Hymnal of the Protestant Episcopal Church* (New York: The Church Pension Fund, 1940), Hymn 44.

FOR CHAPTER 8: *The Source of Our Joy*

[1] William Cowper, *The Hymnal of the Protestant Episcopal Church* (New York: The Church Pension Fund, 1940), Hymn 310. [2] *The Best of G. A. Studdert-Kennedy* (New York: Harper & Brothers, 1948), p. 158. [3] See Leslie D. Weatherhead, *The Resurrection of Christ* (London: Hodder & Stoughton, 1959).

FOR CHAPTER 9: *Assured of Our Victory*

[1] Peter Marshall, *Peter Marshall Speaks* (New York: Caedmon Records, No. 1011). [2] *The Book of Common Prayer* (New York: The Church Pension Fund), p. 80. [3] The writer is indebted to the Right Reverend F. A. Cockin, Bishop of Bristol, and to the late Peter Marshall for ideas expressed in this chapter.

FOR CHAPTER 10: *Climbing the Steep Ascent*

[1] Reginald Heber, *The Hymnal of the Protestant Episcopal Church* (New York: The Church Pension Fund, 1940), Hymn 549.

FOR CHAPTER 11: *Acknowledging Our Double Face*

[1] See Don C. Seitz, *The Tryal of William Penn & William Mead* (Boston: Marshall Jones Company, 1919). [2] Loren C. Eisley, from an unpublished address, "Creativity and Modern Science," given by him at Wainwright House, Rye, New York, at the third seminar on "Science and the Nature of Man" on Oct. 29, 1960. Used by permission.

FOR CHAPTER 12: *Reflecting His Light*

[1] The Collect for Purity, *The Book of Common Prayer* (New York: The Church Pension Fund), p. 67. [2] The article "Pennies from Heaven" appeared in the No. 11, 1958, issue of the periodical *Christian Economics*.

FOR CHAPTER 13: *A Threefold Discipleship*

[1] *The Book of Common Prayer* (New York: The Church Pension Fund), p. 82. [2] Joseph Grigg, *The Hymnal of the Protestant Episcopal Church* (New York: The Church Pension Fund, 1940), Hymn 423.

FOR CHAPTER 14: *The Battlefields of Decision*

[1] W. D. Hyde, *The Hymnal of the Protestant Episcopal Church* (New York: The Church Pension Fund, 1940), Hymn 548. [2] Edited by Helmut Gollwitzer, Reinhold Schneider, and Kathe Kuhn, *Dying We Live* (New York: Pantheon Books, 1956), p. 17. [3] Albert Schweitzer, *The*

Quest of the Historical Jesus (New York: The Macmillan Company, 1910, Eng. trans.), p. 403.

FOR CHAPTER 15: *What Is Expected of Us?*

[1] See Theodore P. Ferris, *This Created World* (New York: Harper & Brothers, 1944). [2] Fulton J. Sheen, *Seven Words to the Cross* (New York: Garden City Press, 1944), p. 21. [3] *Ibid.*, p. 69. [4] Søren Kierkegaard, *Purity of Heart* (New York: Harper & Brothers, 1948).

FOR CHAPTER 16: *Recapturing Lost Radience*

[1] Fyodor Dostoyevsky, *The Brothers Karamazov*, 2 vols.: L 78 and L 79 (Baltimore: Penguin Books), p. 822. [2] Richard Clarke Cabot, "Why I Am a Christian," quoted by George Craig Stewart in *The Faces of Christ* (Milwaukee: Morehouse Publishing Company, 1932), p. 12.

FOR CHAPTER 17: *Showing Him Forth in Our Lives*

[1] From the periodical *Christianity and Crisis*, July 21, 1958. [2] Attributed to St. Francis of Assisi.

FOR CHAPTER 18: *Pitfalls to Avoid*

[1] M. C. D'Arcy, S.J., *The Mind and Heart of Love* (New York: Henry Holt and Company, 1947), p. 54. [2] Dr. Joseph G. Molner, "To Your Good Health," *Providence Evening Bulletin*, July 2, 1963. [3] *New York Times*, Feb. 9, 1964.

FOR CHAPTER 19: *Christ, Our Only Mediator*

[1] H. W. Farrington, *The Hymnal of the Protestant Episco-Church* (New York: The Church Pension Fund, 1940), Hymn 330.

FOR CHAPTER 20:
Hidden Power, Hidden Glory, Hidden Meaning

[1] See "The Wiretapper," *Life* Magazine, June 6, 1957. Film produced by Continental Pictures, Inc. [2] "The Street," produced by Pacific Garden Mission, Chicago, Ill. [3] Samuel Miller, *Now Find the Point Again*, Harvard Divinity School Convocation, Sept. 30, 1958. [4] Elton Trueblood,

The Common Ventures of Life (New York: Harper & Brothers, 1949), p. 86. [5] *The Book of Common Prayer* (New York: The Church Pension Fund), p. 81.

FOR CHAPTER 21: *The Sacrament of Friendship*

[1] John Buchan, *Augustus* (Boston: Houghton Mifflin Company, 1937), p. 39. [2] Bliss Perry, *Park Street Papers* (Boston: Houghton Mifflin Company, 1908), p. 72. [3] Edwin L. Godkin, Presentation Speech of Godkin Lectureship, Harvard University, 1903. [4] Author unknown. Appears in Abingdon Press Anthology (Nashville, Tenn.: Abingdon Press, 1933). [5] From "Christabel," by Samuel Taylor Coleridge. [6] Fritz Kunkel, *In Search of Maturity* (New York: Charles Scribner's Sons, 1946), p. 33. [7] John Fawcett, *The Hymnal of the Protestant Episcopal Church* (New York: The Church Pension Fund), Hymn 495. [8] C. F. Alexander, *The Hymnal of the Protestant Episcopal Church* (New York: The Church Pension Fund, 1940), Hymn 566.